Truly Transformed

DON MATZAT

HARVEST HOUSE PUBLISHERS
Eugene, Oregon 97402

*In memory of Judy LaMorte
who lived and died in Christ Jesus.*

TRULY TRANSFORMED

Copyright © 1992 by Harvest House Publishers
Eugene, Oregon 97402

Library of Congress Cataloging-in-Publication Data

Matzat, Don.
        Truly transformed / Don Matzat.
            p.   cm.
        ISBN 1-56507-019-4
        1. Jesus Christ—Person and offices.   2. Salvation.   3. Christian life—1960– .   I. Title.
        BT202.M379   1992   92-9187
        232—dc20   CIP

Introduction

The Bible clearly teaches that the Christian life is a changed or transformed life. According to the apostle Paul, "If anyone is in Christ, he is a new creation; the old has gone, the new has come!" (2 Corinthians 5:17). We are "transformed into his likeness with ever-increasing glory" (2 Corinthians 3:18), and "transformed by the renewing of our mind" (Romans 12:2). We are "born again" by the "living and enduring Word of God" (1 Peter 1:23). Jesus promised that he came to grant us a full and abundant life (John 10:10).

But what is the nature of this "transformed Christian life"?

I believe that we often make the mistake of focusing primarily upon external behavior. We applaud the likes of gang leader Nicki Cruz, or former Nixon aide Charles Colson, or country-and-western star Johnny Cash, who are able to speak of the dramatic changes that have taken place in their behavior and lifestyle.

While every Christian might desire to have such a glamorous, life-changing testimony and write a bestselling book, for many the best they can offer is: "I used to go to the movies, drink beer, and smoke cigars, but praise Jesus, I've changed! Now I read the Bible, pray every morning, spend five hours in church every week, and watch only Christian television. Glory to God!"

But is this what spiritual transformation is all about? While there is no doubt that the Bible identifies a distinctive Christian lifestyle, it also places greater emphasis upon the transformation of inner attitudes, motives, thoughts, and intentions than upon external behavior. The primary elements of the fruit of the Spirit as described in Galatians 5:22, 23—love, joy, and peace—are matters of the heart and mind. It appears that God is more concerned with what is taking place on the inside than he is with external prohibitions and pious regulations. God truly works "inside-out."

There are many hurting Christians in our world who, because they live fairly decent and responsible lives, are not very anxious about their external behavior. For them, external behavior is not the issue. Their lives fall short of how "real Christians" are supposed to live in the area of relationships, attitudes, emotions, reactions, and inner motives. As a result, they too are filled with guilt and uncertainty.

In addition, they are sick and tired of spiritual charades and playing the role of "good Christians." They are seeking reality. They have had their fill of phonies who talk a good game of holiness but sometimes get caught with their proverbial pants down. They no longer want to sit and listen to pious pontificating preachers who point the accusing finger and stir up guilt and condemnation, but rarely provide explanations as to how real change can take place. They've been disillusioned by quick fixes that offer great expectations but produce no lasting results.

Rarely do you find a person, Christian or otherwise, who doesn't have something wrong with him somewhere. We all have a story to tell about the way life has taken its toll. To find solutions, we may run to counselors and psychologists, read the latest self-help books, embrace secular explanations for our roller coaster emotions, join support groups, and cry on the shoulders of sympathetic friends, yet we may discover that nothing seems to work.

In this book I am dealing with the subject of how God transforms the inner workings of a Christian's life through the supernatural truth in his Word that is revealed to us by his Holy Spirit, thereby producing a "truly transformed" life. I have attempted to set down some very clear principles. God works in our lives in a precise, systematic fashion. He is not the author of confusion.

This book is the result of a 20-year spiritual odyssey which began when I looked at my life and made the observation that there had to be more to Christianity than what I was experiencing. I tried many things, embraced new spiritual experiences, and pursued some of the popular "Christian" notions of the day. But when everything was said and done, the "more" did not turn out to be a *new* list of rules and regulations, or a *new* set of doctrines and beliefs, or even the embracing of *new* spiritual disciplines and practices. Rather, "the more" became a return to the *old* truth that had changed the lives of the great Reformers of the past, men like Martin Luther and John Calvin.

In the light of all the shifting sands of modern evangelicalism, in the aftermath of 20 years of Charismatic confusion, and with modern psychology seeking to redefine some of the basic truths of our faith in order to make room for secular notions, I believe the time has come for Christians to rediscover the dynamic truths clearly taught by the great Reformers. These are not deep, theological truths but the simple understanding of human sin and divine grace. While it is certainly true that Calvin and Luther may have had their points of disagreement, they stood firmly together on the primary issue of the proclamation of sin and grace.

As Protestant Christians, this is our heritage. The proclamation of sin and grace or Law and Gospel changed the lives of millions of people and redirected the course of human history. I hope and pray that reading this book will help you to discover that same truth. Realizing your sin and trusting God's grace can literally transform your life and result in your own personal reformation.

I have many people to thank for their help and input. I especially owe a debt of gratitude to Bob Hawkins Jr. and Eileen Mason at Harvest House for taking all the pieces, putting them together, and pointing me in the right direction. For this I am truly grateful.

—Donald G. Matzat
St. Louis, Missouri

Contents

1

◇

The Verse
That Changed My Life

◇
---

*O*ne evening over 20 years ago a missionary by the name of Russ Cooper shared with me how a New Testament truth had changed his life. Russ had been invited to speak at the meeting of the Ladies' Guild of the congregation in Michigan where I was the pastor. He worked with an organization that made recordings of Bible stories in the native languages of small tribes in Central and South America. He journeyed into many remote locations distributing the recordings.

After he concluded his presentation, I greeted him and thanked him for taking the time to share with us. Curiously, he said to me, "Pastor, I would like to speak with you privately."

So we headed into my office and closed the door. I had no idea what the man wanted and could not figure out why he wanted to speak with me. After sitting down at a table in my office, I asked, "What can I do for you?"

"Well, Pastor," Russ began to explain, "whenever I speak at a church gathering I personally speak with the pastor of the church so that I can share my testimony."

"Oh," I responded, somewhat surprised. I was not accustomed to listening to personal testimonies, but after a brief pause he began to tell me his story.

"I was born and raised in a very legalistic church. I had always wanted to be a good Christian and worked very hard at it. As a result of my striving, I had some real problems with guilt and a sense of failure. I never felt that I was able to measure up. I always lived under condemnation."

"Living under the Law is horrible," I interjected. "Our church focuses upon God's love in Jesus Christ, not upon the Law."

"I'm glad to hear that," Russ responded, somewhat unimpressed. "But I want to tell you, Pastor, about the answer I discovered in the Bible to the problem of living under the Law. You know, most Christians do live under the Law, but the answer to legalism is found in Galatians 2:20. That one verse of the Bible literally changed my life."

"Galatians 2:20? What is that verse?" I asked, attempting to leave the impression that it had merely escaped my memory for the moment.

"In Galatians 2:20 the apostle Paul writes, 'I have been crucified with Christ.'" Russ quoted the verse with a sense of great excitement. "'I no longer live, but Christ lives in me. The life I live in the body I live by faith in the Son of God.' You see," Russ continued, "the Christian life is the result of Christ living his life in me. When I came to know that truth my life was changed. Do you understand what that means?"

"Well, yeah," I began, somewhat defensively. "I have always believed that Jesus lives in my heart."

"Yeah, sure, that's right," Russ affirmed. "But do you know what that *means*? How does the fact that Jesus lives in you affect your day-to-day life?"

I was stumped. I had no testimony to give. I believed that Christ lived in my heart. I had learned that simple truth in Sunday school, but I was unable to answer the question of how that truth affected my day-to-day living.

After a few moments of silence, Russ continued, "Pastor, pursue the meaning of Galatians 2:20. There is a great deal of truth in that verse and throughout the letters of Paul that we have often missed."

We greeted each other, and Russ left.

A few days later Russ called and invited me out to lunch. He gave me a copy of a book by the Chinese evangelist Watchman Nee titled *The Normal Christian Life*. He encouraged me to read it.

Russ would not leave me alone. He visited in our Sunday morning worship service and stayed for Bible class. We continued to meet for lunch. For some reason he felt that I needed to hear the truth of Galatians 2:20.

PRINCIPLE

*Our lives are changed
by God's supernatural truth!*

2

◇

The Search

Begins

◇

I couldn't help but search out Russ Cooper's discovery. The man wouldn't leave me alone. I could not deny that something very real had happened to change his life, nor could I deny that whatever it was, I needed it. At the time I was having severe identity problems. I found myself "playing the role" of the pastor. Since I felt that my life did not measure up to what it meant to be a Christian pastor, I was totally unable to handle criticism. It merely confirmed my self-doubt. Just a few months before, as the result of some of the members of the congregation verbally attacking me, I crumpled into a screaming heap on the living room floor.

I began reading *The Normal Christian Life*. On the very first page Watchman Nee wrote, "God makes it quite clear in his Word that he has only one answer to every human need—his Son Jesus Christ."[1] Nee strongly emphasized that the only way we could experience abundant Christian life was by appropriating the benefits of the cross of Jesus Christ. He demonstrated on the basis of very clear sections of Scripture that the power to live the Christian life was in the cross of Christ, not in our own will, resolutions, or good intentions.

In my mind, I knew the biblical material Nee was quoting. In fact, I was even able to translate the verses from the original Greek language, which was something Russ Cooper was not able to do. But somehow, I didn't *know* the truth in the same way that Russ Cooper knew it. I knew the *doctrinal content* of the Bible verses, but I didn't know what they meant *practically*. They didn't do anything for me, so to speak. I was not able to apply the truth in the Word to my life and have it make a practical difference in the way I lived. Russ Cooper said that these specific portions of Scripture had changed his life. Yet the same material seemingly had no impact upon my life.

At about this same time I had some good friends in our town who had become very interested in and excited about the ministry of the Holy Spirit. One afternoon they stopped in to see me. They shared with me how an evangelist who had visited their Episcopal Church prayed for them to be filled with the Holy Spirit. As a result, the Bible became a new Book. They encouraged me to also pray for the Holy Spirit.

"Perhaps praying for the Holy Spirit was the missing ingredient," I had thought to myself.

So I began to search diligently through the pages of the New Testament, reading and studying all the verses that spoke about the work of the Spirit. I began praying for the Holy Spirit to fill my life. I also continued my quest to understand the testimony of Russ Cooper. What did the apostle Paul mean in Galatians 2:20? What did Jesus mean when he said that he is the Vine and we are the branches? How did this work out in practice?

The Light Begins to Shine

One afternoon, a few months later, I was standing at my patio door looking at the trees in my backyard as I meditated upon the Vine/branch teaching of Jesus. It was wintertime. The variety of oak trees in my yard did not lose their leaves. Instead, their leaves simply turned brown. For all practical purposes, the trees were dead. The thought struck me, "How do those trees get rid of their brown leaves and get new ones?"

I answered my own question by thinking, "They wait until springtime. When the sap comes up out of the roots, it flows into the branches. The old leaves fall off and the new buds appear."

I will never forget that moment; my eyes were opened. Finally I understood what the apostle meant in Galatians 2:20 when he said that I had been crucified with Christ: *The death of Jesus on the cross was my death to sin.* According to Romans 6:11, I was to think of myself as dead to sin and alive to God through Jesus Christ. The Christian life was not "my life," but was the life of Christ Jesus dwelling in me. In the same way that the life of the tree is found in the sap which flows into its branches, so the life of the Christian is found in Christ Jesus who dwells within.

I realized that God had not given me a whole list of things to do and not to do. While the Bible certainly gives many such instructions, God never intended for me to fulfill them by way of willpower and resolutions. God gave me one task: TO ABIDE IN CHRIST JESUS! I had been concerned with getting rid of the old leaves in my life, and I wanted to bear fruit, but I didn't know how to do it. I was trying to shake off the leaves by the use of my own willpower but without success. This produced great frustration. The Holy Spirit then opened my eyes to the truth that I had to stay close to Jesus, and his life in me would do the rest.

But my question was, How do I do it? *How do I stay close to Jesus every day?* Continuing to pray for the Holy Spirit, I carefully studied the New Testament in order to discover the biblical instructions for "abiding in Christ." I had never studied the Bible before seeking an answer to that particular question. As I continued to pray and study, I began to understand. Romans 8:5-8 told me that, if I wanted to experience life and peace, I should set my mind each day upon the things of the Spirit. Philippians 4 spoke to me about rejoicing in the Lord always. Galatians 5 taught me how to identify the fruit of the Spirit and walk in the Spirit.

I realized that God had given me his Word not merely to impart information, but to teach me how to stay close to Jesus. I did not acquire a new set of laws, but I learned some principles for living. For example, I learned that Bible study, prayer, praise, and worship are not merely religious duties, but are means that God has given so that I can abide in the Person of Christ. I learned how to repent and direct my life to Jesus Christ. I gave up trying to be a "good Christian" and consciously sought each day to live in relationship with the Lord Jesus.

A New Awareness

Obviously, there are Christians who have known and put into practice these truths for many years. Perhaps you have known people who sought to live each day in a personal relationship with the Lord Jesus Christ. For example, as I look back, I know that my little Lithuanian grandmother knew what it meant to abide in Christ. It seems to me that every time we arrived at the farmhouse in Connecticut to visit her she was sitting at the dining room table reading and studying her Bible. When working in the kitchen or weeding her garden, she was always singing hymns of praise and thanksgiving. She walked very closely with her Lord, and her life reflected genuine joy, peace, and contentment. She knew what it meant to abide in Christ.

But for me, this was a new awareness which radically changed my life! Now I understood how Russ Cooper could say, "Galatians 2:20 changed my life." The Bible had become a new and exciting book to read. It was amazing—the sections of the New Testament which dealt with the dynamic nature of the Christian life were now alive and meaningful. It was as if the apostle Paul had written his epistles just for me. I knew in my heart that the Person of Jesus Christ was alive and that he really did dwell within me. I experienced for the first time what real peace and joy were all about.

The members of my congregation began to realize that something had happened to their pastor. One Sunday after the service, as I was greeting the people at the church door, one lady said to me, "Pastor, I don't know what happened to you, but you preach about Christ like you know him."

I thought to myself, "I do know him!"

Something had happened to me. The question was, What happened?

PRINCIPLE

It is the work of the Holy Spirit
to open our eyes to the Word of God.

3

◇

*What Happened
to Me?*

◇

Yes, sir, you really got it," my friend Bill said to me one Saturday afternoon; "you really got zapped!" His wife, Joannie, all smiles, sat opposite him at my dining room table. "Jesus really *baptized you in the Holy Spirit*, didn't he? That's great, man!" Bill reached over and grabbed my arm as if to say, "Welcome to the club."

"I know one thing for sure," I happily admitted. "I can't get enough of this Book." I put my hand on the Bible which was next to me on the table. "The Bible has become a new book for me."

"Isn't that an amazing experience?" Bill affirmed. "It seems that things you've read for years without understanding are now alive. The Bible becomes like a little percolator, bubbling up with truth, promises, and blessings. Blubblup, blubblup, blubblup..." Joannie and I laughed at Bill's fish imitation.

"But that's not all, Don; there's a lot more coming," Joannie chimed in. "Now that you're baptized in the Spirit, supernatural things are going to be happening. The miraculous gifts of the Spirit will be a part of your experience. The Holy Spirit will be leading you."

"I'm going to get you some books to read," Bill stated rather matter-of-factly, as if this was now the next obvious step. "It's a new day, my brother, and we are so happy for you."

Charismatic!

I'm sure you've heard something about the Charismatic movement. Most Christian congregations include people who claim to be Charismatics. In recent years the news media have provided a great deal of coverage of some of the antics of the more famous or infamous Charismatics, but of course this news coverage does not characterize all Charismatics. For the most part, they are people who have had a legitimate spiritual awakening in their lives. They love the Lord Jesus, hunger for his Word, and seek to grow in their faith. Specifically, they are identified as Charismatics because they believe that they were baptized in the Holy Spirit and have entered into the supernatural dimension. They claim that as a result of their experience they can experience the gifts of the Spirit and participate in the miracle-working power of God.

I became a Charismatic because I knew of no other way to define or explain what had happened to me. My friends Bill and Joannie, who had told me earlier to seek the Holy Spirit so that I would understand the Bible, were Charismatics. I defined my experience as they had defined their experience. I too believed that I had been baptized in the Holy Spirit.

I was to become a part of the Charismatic movement for the next 15 years. In the first few years I came very close on two or three occasions to getting rebaptized in water and joining one of the Pentecostal Churches. Yet something always seemed to get in the way to stop me, for which I am now truly grateful. After a few years I became recognized as one of the leaders in my denomination's segment of the Charismatic movement.

Teach Me, Lord

During those years I did a great deal of reading and studying. Together with the Bible, I also studied the doctrinal confessions of my church, the writings of the great Reformers Martin Luther and John Calvin, and the theologians who came after the Reformation. There was no doubt that the lives of the Reformers had been transformed. What had happened to them? Were they "baptized in the Holy Spirit"? I was trying to find some way to fit my experience into my theological heritage.

The theologians within my denomination were not very helpful. They did not accept the concept of a "baptism in the Holy Spirit" since it was labeled "Pentecostal." Yet they offered no alternative definition or explanation. While they were quick to point out what *didn't* happen to me, they offered no suggestion as to what *did* happen. It appeared to me, as far as they were concerned, that any spiritual experience or awakening was suspect.

As the years went by, changes began to take place, both in me and in the Charismatic movement itself. I was becoming more and more disenchanted by what I saw in the movement. I simply could not agree with most of the "Charismatic" teachings that I heard. The movement had become "miracle happy." Techniques were being used to seemingly produce miracles that were not biblical. In fact, some of them bordered on silliness and even occultism.

After being in the Charismatic movement for about ten years, I began to critically assess my experiences. While miracles were advertised and promoted, I had never actually seen any. I had never seen a person miraculously healed of an evident affliction. Everyone talked about miracles and had their "pet stories," but nobody had ever actually demonstrated the power to heal or work miracles. Many Charismatics claimed that the Lord was going to do this or the Lord was going to do that, but the Lord never seemed to actually do it. Was the Holy Spirit actually miraculously revealing himself through the gifts of the Spirit, such as speaking in tongues and prophecy? I didn't see it. I heard many so-called "prophets" speaking forth a "word of the Lord" which was a simple paraphrase of a Bible verse. While I believed that biblical "speaking in tongues" involved actual languages, I never knew of one Charismatic "tongue" that was able to be translated. Again I heard stories, but nothing was ever specifically verified.

There was only one real, lasting, undeniable result of my spiritual experience: *The truth in the Word of God had come alive, and as a result my life had changed.* I could not question or deny this fact. This change had actually taken place. Something very real had indeed occurred, but was it "the baptism in the Spirit"?

After a great deal of prayer, study, thought, and inner turmoil, I concluded that I had placed a wrong label upon my spiritual awakening. *I was not baptized in the Holy Spirit!* The Bible never speaks of anyone being baptized in the Holy Spirit. In all of his letters the apostle Paul never mentions the experience. When the four Gospels and the book of Acts do use the phrase "baptize in the Holy Spirit," it is always used to compare the ministry of our Lord Jesus with the ministry of John the Baptist. The Gospel writers were merely demonstrating that the ministry of the Lord Jesus was superior to the ministry of John the Baptist. They were not offering or promising a specific experience called "the baptism in the Holy Spirit" which turns ordinary Christians into supernatural miracle-workers. I had spent 15 years teaching and promoting a false doctrine.

Enlightened!

If I had not been baptized in the Holy Spirit, what had happened to me? How was I to define a dynamic spiritual experience which caused the Bible to become a new and living book to me? There is certainly no doubt that it was the Holy Spirit who was the agent of change within my life. But what label could be applied to his specific work?

In my studies I came across the work of the Spirit called *enlightenment* or *illumination*. Martin Luther, John Calvin, and later Reformation theologians clearly taught the experience of the enlightenment of the Holy Spirit. In Latin, they referred to it as *illuminatio*. In the explanation of the Third Article of the Apostles' Creed, Martin Luther wrote in his *Small Catechism* that the Holy Spirit "calls, gathers, and *enlightens*." In his *Institutes of the Christian Religion*, John Calvin defined enlightenment as taking place "when the Spirit, with a wondrous and special energy, forms the ear to hear and the mind to understand." He also wrote that "whatever is not illuminated by his Spirit is wholly darkness."[1]

In fact, it is safe to say that the Holy Spirit initiated the Protestant Reformation of 1517 through the process of enlightenment. Luther's eyes were supernaturally opened by the Holy Spirit to the truth of justification by faith. This is how he described his experience:

> I felt as if I had been completely reborn and had entered Paradise by widely opened doors. Instantly all Scripture looked different to me.

Again:

> My conscience and spirit were lifted up, and I
> was made certain that it is the righteousness of
> God which justifies and saves us. And imme-
> diately these words became sweet and delight-
> ful to me. This is what the Holy Spirit taught
> me. . . .[2]

The Methodist Church finds its beginning in the
enlightenment of John Wesley. At the famous meeting of
the Aldersgate Literary Society in 1738, during the reading of Luther's commentary on Paul's epistle to the
Romans, Wesley claimed that "his heart was strangely
warmed."

In comparing my eye-opening experience with the
definitions of enlightenment offered by various Reformation theologians, I discovered a perfect match. I
concluded that enlightenment was the proper label for
my spiritual awakening. As a result of the enlightenment of the Holy Spirit, verses of Scripture which had
previously been obscure and meaningless were now
very clear and practical. My life had been changed, not
by an unusual mystical experience, but by the living,
Word of God becoming real in my life.

Because I now correctly redefined my experience as
being the *enlightenment of the Holy Spirit* and not *the baptism in the Spirit,* I no longer had any reason to remain in
the Charismatic movement. There was no longer a
unique doctrine that I was trying to promote. I discovered that basic Protestant Reformation theology included
the experience of the enlightenment of the Holy Spirit,
even though this important truth had not been properly
emphasized or explained.

In the fall of 1986 I renounced my involvement in the
Charismatic movement. This was a very difficult deci-
sion to make, for 15 years I had been identified as "a
Charismatic." My life and ministry had revolved around

that identification. In addition, I had formed many precious relationships and friendships over those 15 years.

While my relationships with some of my Charismatic friends grew cold, my relationship with my Lord Jesus grew stronger. My experience of new life, joy, and peace was now built upon the solid foundation of biblical truth. I was not baptized in the Holy Spirit. Rather, I had been enlightened by the Holy Spirit.

PRINCIPLE

The combination of studying God's Word
and praying for the Holy Spirit will produce
life-changing results.

4

◇

*A Rose
by Any Other Name*

◇

*P*erhaps some of you are thinking, "You're splitting hairs. Who cares how you define an experience with the Holy Spirit as long as you receive the benefits from the experience? What difference does it make how you label it? After all, as Shakespeare put it, 'a rose by any other name smells as sweet.'"

While the words of Shakespeare might apply to roses, they certainly do not apply to biblical theology. How we define the way the Holy Spirit works in order to produce an abundant life through Jesus Christ is vitally important. It is through the truth that we draw from the Word of God that the Holy Spirit changes our lives. Properly defining that truth determines what we expect from God. The content and parameters of our faith will be formed by our theological definitions. Jesus said, "You will know the truth, and the truth will make you free."

For example, a program that is purchased for a computer will come with an instruction manual. If we are to receive the full benefit of the program, we must take the time to find out how it works by reading the instructions. In the same way, if we are to receive the full benefit of what God has accomplished for us in Christ Jesus, we must find out how "the abundant life program" works. Of course, in the Bible, God has provided the instruction manual.

If we embrace theological error and distortion, the affect upon our lives will be negative. We will readily become discouraged and disillusioned if our day-to-day experiences do not agree with our spiritual expectations. I believe that the guilt and condemnation, and the lack of joy, peace, and contentment experienced by many Christians today is the result of embracing wrong theological definitions.

Let me give you some examples.

Distortions

There are Christians today who believe that all negative experiences are the work of the devil. They define "negative experiences" as those circumstances which do not make them happy, successful, or prosperous. From their perspective, God is in the business of blessing them and the devil is in the business of making them miserable. They mistakenly believe that Jesus took upon himself the dealings of God and left us with only divine blessings. If they bind the devil and claim the blessings, they believe that success and prosperity is right around the corner. Is this good theology?

The Bible makes it very clear that God disciplines those whom he loves. The negative experiences of life are a part of God's program for changing our lives and producing in us spiritual growth and maturity. The apostle Paul boasted of his weaknesses so that the power of Christ might rest upon him.

Those who embrace this wrong theological definition never grow up spiritually. They remain spoiled little children who continually seek to move the hand of God and get God to bless them and give them what they want. When faced with problems that they are not able to overcome, they think they are not binding the devil correctly, or that they do not have enough faith in their faith, or that they are not speaking the right words against their negative experiences. This failure produces guilt and condemnation which are directly related to their wrong definition.

Further, there are Christians who hold a distorted understanding of human nature. They believe that their old sinful nature was eliminated when they were saved or born again. If they should fall into sin, it is not their fault; the devil made them do it.

Wrong definitions produce wrong expectations. We easily become disillusioned if what we expect is not what we get. We might eventually be prone to reject Christianity entirely.

Many examples could be offered to demonstrate that distorted theological definitions pervert the Christian life and experience. When dealing with theology, *a rose by any other name does not smell as sweet!*

Seeking Miracles

Those who believe that they had a spiritual experience called "the baptism in the Holy Spirit," and as a result were ushered into the supernatural dimension, focus their attention upon miracles. If an emotional problem or a besetting sin exists, rather than standing upon the promises in the Word of God, they all too often seek a "quick fix" and a supernatural solution. It is very understandable that many Charismatics embrace the distorted practices of casting out demons, inner healing, slaying in the Spirit, healing the family tree, Jungian psychology, and visualization. It is also understandable that some of the most popular Charismatic ministers are not those who powerfully preach the Gospel but those who claim to produce miracles of healing.

When I was a Charismatic, I believed that I was baptized in the Holy Spirit and was now moving in a supernatural dimension. I expected to do the works that Jesus and the first-century apostles did. This included working miracles, casting out demons, and healing the sick. Yet no matter how fervently I prayed, or pleaded, or claimed, or commanded miracles in the name of Jesus, nothing ever happened. There either had to be something wrong with me, or for some reason God was not cooperating with my expectations.

My purpose in pointing this out to you is not to come against sincere Charismatics and Pentecostals, even though it is necessary to point out their incorrect theology on certain issues. My purpose is to seek the proper understanding of truth that will not lead to disillusionment. When I redefined my spiritual awakening as being the enlightenment of the Holy Spirit I was directed to the Word of God, not to the pursuit of miracles! As a result, I was no longer disappointed. I was receiving from the Holy Spirit exactly what I expected to receive— a growing personal relationship with the Lord Jesus, the practical application of biblical promises to my life, and the strengthening of my faith. As a pastor, my preaching and teaching became far more effective. In addition, a great burden was lifted from me: I was no longer under pressure to try to perform as an alleged miracle-working Charismatic.

If you are a Charismatic and have become increasingly disillusioned by the unfulfilled claims of the movement, please allow me to offer a word of encouragement: *Do not reject the spiritual awakening that has taken place in your life.*

Rather, *redefine* that awakening. You have not been disappointed by the Holy Spirit; you have been disappointed by those, possibly including myself, who might have given you a wrong definition of the working of the Holy Spirit. You were not baptized in the Holy Spirit. The Holy Spirit opened your eyes to the truth that is contained in the Word of God. It was the *Word of God* that changed your life. Look for Jesus where he has promised to meet you: in his Word.

Clear Definitions Are Very Important

I cannot impress upon you enough the importance of seeking and maintaining clear, precise definitions for the way God works, especially if a spiritual experience is involved. Believing a distorted theological definition will hinder your Christian growth. Do not make the mistake of thinking that Christian doctrine and Christian experience are in opposition. While it is true that true doctrine without experience will produce a dead dogmatism, a legitimate Christian experience without clear definition will lead to chaos.

Some years ago a group of Charismatic Lutheran pastors and theologians gathered together for the specific purpose of formulating a clear, concise definition for "the baptism in the Holy Spirit." They soon discovered that they were unable to arrive at an agreement. The project was eventually scrapped. They explained the failure by suggesting that the Holy Spirit works in a mysterious fashion and that the experience of the baptism in the Holy Spirit was not able to be clearly defined. As one man put it, "We have Jesus; who needs theology?"

Many Charismatic leaders have manifested a very sloppy and irresponsible attitude toward theological definitions. They claim that they do not want to be divisive by defining their theology too precisely. In the name of "love" and acceptance of the brethren, they minimize the importance of maintaining clear definitions and speaking out against error. The result of this has been clearly demonstrated over the past two decades. A movement which is characterized by chaotic theology will succeed in producing little more than chaos. In addition, many of the "little people" have been disillusioned, disheartened, and spiritually injured by these irresponsible leaders.

God is not the author of confusion. The "baptism in the Holy Spirit" was nondefinable because it is nonexistent. If the experience was clearly taught in the Bible, it could be readily defined by the Bible.

Of course, providing a clear, precise definition of the enlightenment of the Holy Spirit is also very necessary. And this is what I hope to do.

PRINCIPLE

Seeking and maintaining clear,
precise definitions for Christian truth,
especially when personal spiritual experience
is involved, is vital for your spiritual life and growth.
God is not the author of theological confusion.

5

*Enlightened by the
Holy Spirit*

G ood morning!" Anna Meier joyfully greeted me at the door of the church after the Sunday morning worship. Anna, who was normally a quiet and collected person, seemed rather excited.

"Pastor, I have to tell you that was a great sermon. It was eye-opening. It was fantastic. I had never heard that before." Anna paused and with a sense of relief continued, "It is really good to know that I am right with God."

I was taken back by Anna's statement. I did not feel that my sermon that particular Sunday was much different in style and content from what I preached every Sunday. It was Reformation Sunday, and I preached on the usual theme of justification by faith. I explained to my congregation that our right standing with God was not based upon our good works or obedience to the Law, but upon the righteousness of Christ Jesus.

I knew that Anna had been a member of the congregation all her life, which was about 65 years. She had heard many sermons on the theme of justification by faith, yet she claimed she had not heard. Why hadn't she heard? Had all these sermons simply gone in one ear and out the other?

Following Anna's enlightenment, she became a different person. She shared with me at a small group Bible study that she had always believed that she was going to heaven because she obeyed the Ten Commandments. As a result of her understanding of the truth about justification, her life reflected much greater peace and joy.

What happened to Anna Meier on that particular Sunday morning so that she finally heard and understood?

The Mysterious Human Mind

The human mind is a strange and mysterious thing. It has tremendous capabilities. It can know, understand, feel, think, reason, determine, remember, invent, and discover. Great minds are capable of grasping incredible concepts and solving complicated problems. Yet for less-trained minds, certain concepts are beyond their limits. I remember trying to explain the workings of a computer to my 85-year-old father. He interrupted my explanation by saying, "Donald, forget it. It's beyond me!"

There are times when the mind is "enlightened," or a person has what psychologists call an "aha experience." Something finally clicks, and what previously had been cloudy and obscure is now clear and able to be understood.

According to the dictionary, to enlighten means "to give to the mind revealing or broadening knowledge," or "to give the light of truth." Enlightenment is the illumination of the mind by which the "eyes of the understanding" are opened. As a result, a problem finds a solution. A puzzling concept is finally understood. A good idea begins to emerge. Cartoonists usually depict enlightenment by drawing the picture of an illumined light bulb.

When I was a freshman in high school I had the hardest time understanding the "factoring" of algebraic equations. The concept just didn't register with me. I still remember the evening while doing my algebra homework that I received a flash of insight. My mind sorted out all the information, and suddenly everything fit together and the concepts became clear. After "being enlightened," I could "factor" anything no matter how many "x's" or "y's" were in the equation. The light bulb went on! My mind was illumined or "enlightened."

Simple psychological enlightenment causes your eyes to look at something in a new and different way. You are all familiar with optical illusions. Perhaps some of you have seen the inkblot picture of the face of Christ. When you look at the picture, all you see is a mass of inkblots. But all of a sudden the light goes on and you clearly see the face of Christ. After being "enlightened," every time you look at the picture all you see is the face of Christ. Those who remain "in the dark" and only perceive ink-blots become the objects of your instruction.

"See, here's the eyes. Here's the nose, the chin... don't you see it?" you explain. "Look carefully. Do you see the face of Christ?"

"No, I don't see it!"

"What's wrong with you?" you ask impatiently. "It's so clear!"

Those who are enlightened often demonstrate little patience toward those who still remain "in the dark."

But in addition to being a simple mental or psychological phenomenon, enlightenment can be caused by the influence of outside spiritual forces.

An Occult Concept

The experience of spiritual "enlightenment" or "illumination" is a very popular subject today among both advocates of the New Age occultism and promoters of Eastern religions. Noted actress Shirley MacLaine, in her books on New Age teaching, encourages us to seek within ourselves to discover divine light. Modern mystics and gurus refer to the "inner illumination of the soul." Hindus speak of their "enlightened masters." In fact, they even refer to Jesus as being one of those "enlightened masters." Those who engage in occult meditation and visualization claim to open the "third eye" to generate spiritual illumination. Some claim that there is a group of powerful men who have arrived at the highest levels of the Masonic Order. Their alleged purpose is to exercise control over this world. They call themselves "the Illuminati," or the enlightened ones.

According to modern mystics and occultists, the result of enlightenment or illumination is a deeper spiritual knowledge and understanding. Numerous explanations are offered for these claims. One of the concepts of the depth psychology of Dr. Carl Jung is that the unconscious mind is the source of deeper knowledge and provides enlightened and creative thoughts. According to the popular "Mind Control" concepts of Jose Silva, "spirit guides" enlighten the mind with greater knowledge and understanding. Eastern mystics claim to receive divine revelation by the direct illumination of the soul

New Age occult enlightenment is very dangerous. It does not occur as the result of harmless psychological techniques. Occultists and mystics are not simply playing mind-games. Anytime a person seeks supernatural wisdom and insight by meditating and looking within themselves or imploring the aid of "spirit guides," you can be very sure that the devil is involved! The Bible clearly tells us that the spiritual reality behind all occult mystical experiences is demonic (see Deuteronomy 18:9-13 and Acts 16:16-18). Because of the very popular occult usage of the term "enlightenment," one might readily conclude that it is a "bad word" for Christians. A book about spiritual enlightenment might be construed as a promotion of New Age occultism. But let me assure you, this is not the case!

A Biblical Concept

While it is true that spiritual enlightenment is promoted by occultists and mystics, the fact of the matter is that to enlighten the mind is also a genuine work of the Holy Spirit. Christians who experience the enlightenment of the Holy Spirit and have their eyes opened to an important biblical truth are not occultists. Because the experience of spiritual enlightenment has been stolen by the devil and is being promoted by occultists does not mean that we should avoid it. Rather, we should seek to explore and understand the *biblical* concept. The Holy Spirit's work of enlightenment must be of great importance for Christians, since the devil never steals from God or perverts a work of the Holy Spirit that has little or no value.

Enlightenment is first and foremost a biblical concept. The Bible tells us that Jesus supernaturally *opened the minds of his disciples* so that they would understand the Scriptures (Luke 24:47). The apostle Paul prayed for the enlightenment of the Christians who were a part of the church at Ephesus (Ephesians 1:15-18). Read carefully what he wrote:

> Ever since I heard about your faith in the Lord Jesus and your love for all the saints, I have not stopped giving thanks for you, remembering you in my prayers. I keep asking that the God

of our Lord Jesus Christ, the glorious Father,
may give you the Spirit of wisdom and revelation so that you may know him better. I pray
also that the eyes of your heart may be enlightened in order that you may know the hope to
which he has called you.

In Romans 12:1,2 the apostle Paul teaches that real
transformation takes place in our lives as a result of our
minds being renewed. "Do not conform any longer to
the pattern of this world," he writes, "but be transformed by the renewing of your mind." The mind that
has been enlightened by the Holy Spirit is programmed
by the truth of God's Word and promises. As a result, the
life is changed.

There is no doubt, according to Scripture, that our
behavior is directly affected by the truth that fills our
minds. In defining the biblical understanding of the
mind, Edward T. Welch says that the mind is "the initia-
tor of the ethical drama of life."[1] Dr. William Backus
states that "the Bible solidly teaches that man's feelings,
passions and behavior are subject to and conditioned by
the way he thinks."[2]

The Holy Spirit and the Bible

As you see, the concept of enlightenment is used in
different contexts and is subject to various definitions.
Enlightenment can be a simple psychological experi-
ence. Enlightenment can be a demonic, occult experience.
Enlightenment can be a genuine, biblical work of the
Holy Spirit.

The question is, How can we know the difference?
Perhaps my experience of enlightenment in which I
came to understand the meaning of Galatians 2:20 was
no different from the experiences taught by New Age
occultists. If we seek the experience of spiritual enlightenment, how can we be sure that we will not be deceived?

There is a great difference between occult enlightenment and the enlightenment of the Holy Spirit, and the difference is not difficult to discern. The method for gaining Christian enlightenment has been clearly defined by Reformation theologians of the past who were forced to confront the occultism of their age. They concluded that *the Holy Spirit enlightens the mind that is actively engaged in studying and meditating upon the Word of God, the Bible.* The purpose of the enlightenment of the Holy Spirit is always directed at faith in the Lord Jesus Christ.

Whereas mystics and occultists seek enlightenment by emptying the mind of all thoughts and waiting passively for the "spirit" to move in order to gain spiritual revelations, the enlightened Christian mind is not an empty mind. The Holy Spirit enlightens the person who is seeking Jesus and studying and actively meditating upon his Word. The subject matter which the Christian grasps by way of enlightenment is not arbitrary. The Holy Spirit will not reveal to us some new, unique truths about Jesus. He enlightens to our understanding *that which has already been revealed in the Bible.* While it is true that only the Holy Spirit can teach us about Jesus, it is also true that *the Bible is his only textbook.*

After the Reformation of 1517 there were some Protestants who taught that God illumines and enlightens the mind directly, apart from and without the Bible. They were called "enthusiasts." Many of these "new prophets" actually scoffed at the Bible. Martin Luther strongly spoke against them and declared, "Whatever spirit comes to us without the external Word of God is the devil." From Luther's perspective, any experience of spiritual enlightenment that is not joined to the Bible is from the devil.

We still have many "enthusiasts" in the church today who claim to gain knowledge directly from "the spirit." For example, one day I heard a woman say, "When I experienced the Holy Spirit, I knew that Jesus was my Lord."

"That's not true," I responded.

"Oh, yes it is," she argued. "When the Holy Spirit filled my life he assured me that Jesus was ruling over this world. He is my Lord."

"You know that Jesus is your Lord because the Bible says he is," I explained. "What the Holy Spirit did was to enlighten your understanding of that Word."

"Well, yes, of course," she admitted. "But I do know that he is my Lord."

This is not simply a "play on words" or "hairsplitting." It is vitally important for us to affirm that Christian knowledge and faith comes from the Word of God, the Bible. But if we are asked the question "How do we acquire that knowledge and faith?" we affirm, "not by use of reason or senses, intelligence or education, but by the gracious enlightenment of the Holy Spirit."

It is the will of God for all Christians to grow and thereby change. The apostle Peter wrote, "Like newborn babies, crave pure spiritual milk, so that by it you may grow up in your salvation" (1 Peter 2:2). The "pure spiritual milk" is the Word of God, the Bible. God desires for us to "crave" his Word and thereby grow in our Christian knowledge, understanding, and faith.

Such growth can take place only through the ongoing enlightenment of the Holy Spirit. Without the enlightenment of the Holy Spirit, we do not and cannot understand the Bible, because the Bible is a very unique book!

PRINCIPLE

The enlightenment of the Holy Spirit is a Christian experience clearly taught in the Bible. The Holy Spirit enlightens the mind that is engaged in reading, studying, and meditating upon God's Word and promises.

6

◇

Inspiration
and Enlightenment

◇

A couple of years ago I decided to telephone most of the faithful members of my congregation and invite them to come to Sunday morning Bible class. A number of my phone calls went something like this.

"I'm calling to invite you to attend the Sunday morning Bible class," I explained. "We meet between the services, coffee is served, and I would sure love to have you there."

For a few moments there was no response. Finally the voice on the other end said, "No, Bible class is not for me. Thank you for inviting me, Pastor, but I really don't understand the Bible. I'll come to church every Sunday, but please don't ask me to come to Bible class."

"That's the purpose of Bible class," I explained. "Let me help you . . ."

"No," he interrupted. "I'm just not interested. It is your job as the Pastor to understand the Bible. I'll listen to your sermons."

There are many Christians who hold the wrong impression that understanding of the Bible is reserved for clergy, Bible students, and theologians. They think that pastors go to seminary to study the Bible in the same way doctors go to medical school to study their medical texts and lawyers study their volumes of legal precedent.

For this reason, it is not strange that so many hurting Christians run after quick-fix spiritual experiences, put so much confidence in spiritual leaders, or seek secular psychological solutions for their problems. If the Bible is not a living book for them and if they do not know how to receive benefits from it, they have no other alternatives.

The Bible was not written for trained theologians and clergymen. The words of the Bible are not so deep and intellectual that a common person is not able to understand them. God most certainly would not offer his promises and benefits to this world in words that could not be understood.

Yet there is something truly unique about the words of the Bible which does leave the impression that they are beyond the understanding of the average person. But this has nothing to do with whether or not a person has a theological education. The words of the Bible, while not difficult words, are words inspired by the Holy Spirit.

Inspired by the Holy Spirit

The words of the Bible do not merely communicate human thoughts, memories, and instructions. If you want to understand the words and promises of God, you cannot read the Bible in the same way you would read a novel or a history text. While the words of the Bible in and of themselves are not difficult, they are words that were written under the direct influence of the Holy Spirit. God himself communicates to us through the words of the Bible. The Holy Spirit inspired the very words and thoughts that were recorded by these sacred writers.

How do we know this?

The Bible itself witnesses to the divine inspiration of the writers. Peter tells us that "men spoke from God as they were carried along by the Holy Spirit." Paul writes to Timothy: "All Scripture is God-breathed."

For this reason, the words of the Bible are God's powerful words which cause results to take place in the lives of people. The Bible is a supernatural book. It produces supernatural results. It is very understandable that when my eyes were opened to the meaning of Galatians 2:20 and when I grasped the truth that Jesus is the Vine and I am a branch, my life was changed. It is very understandable that Anna Meier became a new person when her eyes were opened to justification by faith. It is also very understandable that all legitimate reformations and renewals that have taken place in the church were caused by the Holy Spirit opening believers' eyes to the Word and promises of God. It is also very understandable that the concept of enlightenment has been distorted by the devil!

When God created the heavens and the earth, he merely spoke the words. When our Lord Jesus healed people of their afflictions, he merely spoke the words. God works through *words*. The words of the Bible are God's powerful supernatural words.

The apostle Paul describes the words of the Gospel of Jesus Christ as being "the power of God" (Romans 1:16). The Greek word which is translated power is *dunamis*, from which we derive the English word "dynamite." We might say that the words of the Bible are "dynamite" words which release the very power of God. In order for this to take place, the Holy Spirit had to inspire the human writers.

Therefore, if you do not understand the Bible, this does not mean that there is something theologically technical and lofty about the words of the Bible, nor does it mean that there is something wrong with you. What it *does* mean is that your natural mind is not in tune with the mind of the Spirit. You need to be enlightened. If the human authors of the Bible were *inspired* by the Holy Spirit, must it not follow that the readers of the Bible, if they are to understand, must be *enlightened* by the same Holy Spirit?

Inspiration of the writer demands the enlightenment of the reader. If, for example, an author writes in English, you have to be able to read Enlglish to understand him. If the words are written in Greek, you have to be able to read Greek. If the author writes using a certain code, you have to be familiar with the code. But if the author writes under the direct influence and inspiration of the Holy Spirit, you must be influenced and enlightened by the same Holy Spirit in order to understand the meaning of the words and receive the benefits they offer.

Natural knowledge, reason, and intelligence, while being valuable gifts from God, will not comprehend the Holy Spirit's supernatural truth. While our natural intelligence may help us to study the biblical words, understand the social and historical context in which they were written, and translate the original biblical languages, only the Holy Spirit can communicate to us the benefits contained in God's powerful words and thereby change our lives. Martin Luther wrote:

> All men have a darkened heart, so even if they know how to tell and present all that Scripture contains, yet they are unable to feel and truly know it.[1]

AM or FM?

Think of it in this way: A radio station transmits words and sounds into the air. Some of the words are AM words while others are FM words. This has to do with the way in which the words or sounds are modulated or regulated as they are transmitted. Some are regulated by their amplitude or size. This is called AM. Others are regulated by their frequency. This is called FM. In order to receive these words and hear them, you must have a "receiver." Some receivers will accept FM words and others will accept AM words. If you have an AM radio you cannot receive FM sounds. They are simply not compatible.

In the same way, the Bible speaks of two dimensions in this world. There is a "natural" dimension and a "spiritual" dimension. The natural dimension relates to basic human life. The biblical Greek word that is translated "natural" is *psychikos* or pertaining to the human mind. From this word we get "psychology," which is a study of the natural human mind. The truths of history or science or mathematics are natural truths. They are grasped by the natural capabilities of the human mind.

The words of the Bible are not a part of that natural dimension but are a part of the spiritual dimension. While there is of course a natural dimension to the Bible in that it deals with facts of history and is written in human language, in order for spiritual knowledge and understanding to be gained and spiritual benefits to be received from the Bible, the mind of the reader has to be enlightened, or illuminated, by the Holy Spirit. Without his gracious enlightenment we are doomed to say, "I don't understand the Bible."

Confused Disciples

The disciples of our Lord Jesus Christ had the same problem in understanding the teachings of their Master.

They were often confused as to his ministry and purposes, even though he clearly explained himself, using all kinds of parables and illustrations. Their minds had to be opened. Their eyes had to be enlightened.

In Matthew 16 we have some beautiful examples of the disciples and their understanding of what Jesus taught them. Read the chapter.

In verses 5-12 we read about Jesus and his disciples together in a boat crossing the Sea of Galilee. Jesus had just confronted the Pharisees and Sadducees. He wanted to warn his disciples about the pride-filled attitude and teachings of these religious leaders so he said to them, "Be on your guard against the yeast of the Pharisees and the Sadducees."

"What does he mean by 'the yeast of the Pharisees and Sadducees'?" the disciples asked each other.

Finally, after discussing it among themselves, they arrived at the conclusion that Jesus had to be referring to the fact that they had forgotten to bring bread with them for lunch. After all, they reasoned, what else could he mean by "yeast"?

The disciples' interpretation of the words of Jesus seems incredible, especially in light of the fact that this incident took place immediately following the feeding of the four thousand. Before their eyes, Jesus had taken seven loaves of bread and had fed them all. He certainly would not be concerned about lunch! How could they have so badly misinterpreted the words of Jesus?

In the very next section of Matthew 16, verses 13-20, we read about Peter's wonderful confession that Jesus is the Christ, the Son of the living God. Peter's eyes had been opened to the Person of the Christ. Jesus commended Peter: "This was not revealed to you by any man, but by my Father in heaven."

Continuing with verses 21-23, we see another shift. This time Peter revealed his spiritual blindness. Jesus told his disciples that he was going to go to Jerusalem, and that there he would suffer, die, and be raised from the dead. Peter took Jesus aside and said, "This is not going to happen to you!"

Jesus responded to Peter by saying, "Get behind me, Satan!"

While Peter professed that Jesus was the Christ or the Messiah, he had no idea of his mission.

Many times throughout the Gospels we are confronted with the confusion of the disciples. Like many Christians today, they too did not understand much of what Jesus was trying to communicate to them. Even though they saw him in the flesh and heard his teachings, they still did not fully understand who he was, why he came, and where he was going.

Why No Understanding?

Jesus had spent a great deal of time with his disciples. He had shared his heart with them, explaining to them the ways and purposes of God. Yet on many occasions the disciples did not understand him. He had told them very plainly about himself and his Father in heaven, but for some reason his words did not register with them. Their minds did not comprehend. They could not see.

Why? What was wrong with these disciples that they did not understand? Was Jesus so much more intelligent than they were? Was he speaking brilliant words that were so theologically technical that these poor, untrained disciples remained in the dark? Did Jesus merely come into this world to speak mysterious words which no one could understand?

Certainly not! There was more to it than that. There was something unique about the words of Jesus. They were not like ordinary human words, which are able to be grasped and comprehended by the unaided human intellect. The words of Jesus were not intended merely to impart information, discuss facts, or share feelings. *His words produced spiritual life.* Spiritual benefits were imparted through his words. In his discourse on the Bread of Life recorded in the sixth chapter of John, Jesus said that the words he spoke were "spirit and life." In the upper room he told his disciples that they had been "made clean" by the words which he had spoken to them. His words were not merely spoken in order to explain various truths to his disciples so that they could understand with their minds. His words possessed a spiritual dynamic.

Consider the effects of the words of our Lord Jesus. The lives of people were changed by his words. Demons screamed when he spoke. People were healed by his words. He spoke to the winds and the waves, and they obeyed him. He told Peter to walk on the water, and Peter did. The woman caught in adultery was changed when he said, "Go and sin no more." The people were amazed when he taught, because he spoke as one having authority. The centurion at Capernaum knew that Jesus merely had to speak a word and his servant would be healed. The words of Jesus were not ordinary words at all. They possessed spiritual power.

The disciples were having difficulty receiving the words of Jesus because they were not spiritually in tune with him. Their minds did not comprehend the spiritual truths which Jesus spoke. They were not equipped to hear and receive what Jesus was talking about. Something inside them had to be adjusted before they could understand. Jesus was speaking AM words and they were equipped with FM receivers. In order for them to receive and understand spiritual insight and understanding, their minds had to enlightened, or illuminated. Their eyes had to be opened!

Their Eyes Were Opened

After Jesus rose from the dead, on Easter evening he caught up with two of his disciples who were heading home to Emmaus after celebrating the Passover in Jerusalem. But even though they were followers of Jesus, they did not recognize him. They were very upset by the events that had taken place in Jerusalem. Their Lord and Master had been put to death, and they were discussing these events. Jesus, who was a stranger to them, explained to them from the Old Testament that these events were necessary. It was God's intention for his Messiah to suffer and to die.

When they arrived at Emmaus, since it was evening, they invited this Stranger to spend the night with them. At the supper table Jesus broke the bread and gave it to them. At that point *their eyes were opened*. They saw him. They recognized him as being Jesus. He then disappeared from their sight.

In some miraculous fashion Jesus caused the eyes, the minds, and the hearts of these disciples to become spiritual "receivers." They said to each other, "Were not our hearts burning within us while he talked with us on the road and opened the Scriptures to us?"

He Opened Their Minds

This same type of eye-opening experience took place with all the disciples of Jesus immediately before he ascended into heaven. Jesus gathered his disciples together and taught them from the Scriptures that it was necessary for him to suffer and die so that repentance and the forgiveness of sins would be preached to all people. In Luke 24:45 we read this simple yet startling verse: *"Then he opened their minds so they could understand the Scriptures."*

He opened their minds! It was a miracle! Jesus enabled his disciples to understand, and it produced great results.

On the Day of Pentecost, when the Holy Spirit became the permanent resident within the church, Peter preached a sermon from the Old Testament which he now understood. He explained to the people about the ministry of the Messiah, proving from the Scriptures that Jesus was the Christ, the Lord, the Savior, the very Son of God himself. He preached with power and conviction. As a result, 3000 people were converted.

The disciples finally understood what God had accomplished through the death and resurrection of Jesus Christ, because Jesus himself had opened their eyes, their minds, and their hearts to his Word. They were enlightened!

PRINCIPLE

*Since "holy men of God" wrote
the words of the Bible under the inspiration
of the Holy Spirit, "holy people of God"
can only comprehend those words through the
enlightenment of the Holy Spirit.*

7

◇

Ask, and It
Shall Be Given You!

◇

*H*ow do we receive the enlightenment of the Holy Spirit? Are their steps involved? Is there a preparation that we are expected to make? Mystics and occultists empty their minds of all thoughts and wait in silence for their demonic spiritual illumination. How does the Christian attain the genuine enlightenment of the Holy Spirit? Are there preparations that we should make before the Holy Spirit will enlighten our understanding of the divine Word?

Even though we are Christians and the Holy Spirit dwells within us, our natural sinful human nature remains an enemy of God. Our natural minds are "darkened." The apostle Paul tells us that our sinful nature is in conflict with the desires of the Spirit, and the Spirit is in conflict with the desires of the sinful human nature (Galatians 5:17). While the Holy Spirit desires to enlighten our minds, our sinful human nature is opposed to the light of the Holy Spirit. So it is the Holy Spirit himself who urges us, "Seek my light! Desire my enlightenment! Learn from me!"

In studying the subject of the enlightenment of the Holy Spirit, I discovered that most theologians who deal with it speak of prayer as a necessary preparation for receiving enlightenment. One eighteenth-century teacher of the Bible referred to prayer as an "auxiliary" or accessory or partner to the enlightenment of the Holy Spirit.[1] Another theologian wrote:

> Just as no one can see the sun without the sun, no one can know God without God, without divine illumination. . . . The Scriptures are not understood in a beneficial way without the Spirit by whom they were brought about; we must daily implore his grace and enlightenment by our prayers.[2]

Praying that the Holy Spirit will open our eyes to the truth that is revealed in the Bible is a very important but often neglected practice. We should approach the Word of God with the recognition that we are dealing with *God's Word*. The Bible is unlike any other book. As we discussed before, the Bible is a supernatural book which cannot be grasped by mere natural reason.

The Purpose of Praying for Enlightenment

Perhaps some of you are asking, "Since the Holy Spirit is intimately joined to the Bible, why is it necessary for us to pray? Shouldn't the enlightenment of the Spirit take place automatically, as we read the Bible, without our prayer?"

By urging us to pray, the Holy Spirit is turning us away from our natural understanding so that, in seeking his gracious enlightenment, we might gain life-affecting truth from his Word. By following the urgings of the Spirit to pray, we are put in a position to receive from the Holy Spirit.

To pick up on an illustration that I used earlier, I think of prayer for the enlightenment of the Holy Spirit as switching the radio dial from AM to FM. It places us into a different mode, so to speak, so that we are tuned in to the Holy Spirit's frequency.

There are many times when it is necessary for us to switch modes. For example, to arrive home after a harried day at the office, fighting traffic all the way, or to finally finish the dishes and get the kids to bed, and to then sit down and pick up your Bible and immediately expect to be spiritually fed by the Holy Spirit is not feasible. The influences of the devil, the world, and our own sinful nature put us out of touch with the Holy Spirit. We all too easily get caught up in the things of this world, or turn our attention upon ourselves. So the Holy Spirit prompts us to switch modes, to turn our hearts and minds toward God so that we might become ready receivers of his grace. Worship will produce the same effect, especially if we sing hymns of praise that contain good scriptural content.

The important thing to keep in mind is that our prayer or praise does not *cause* the Holy Spirit to come and enlighten our understanding of the Word of God. The Holy Spirit is always present where the Word of God is found. Prayer or praise *changes our hearts and directs our minds unto God* so that we might receive from him.

I Forgot to Pray!

Because of our old sinful nature, our willingness to obey the promptings of the Spirit to pray, to worship and praise, and to seek and desire our God is often quite feeble. By nature we are proud people and do not want to express our dependency upon God. So we need to be continually reminded.

Just about every Saturday evening I have the same experience. Through the course of the week I do some reading and studying in preparation for my Sunday morning sermon, but putting the thoughts together is reserved for Saturday night.

So, seated on the sofa in my study, I begin to think about the text, the theme for the day, and try to come up with some good ideas that I can preach. Very often there is a struggle involved; nothing seems to fit together. Finally the thought hits me, "You haven't prayed for enlightenment."

My first reaction to the thought is embarrassment. Why have I forgotten to pray? Why does this same failure happen week after week? So I repent or change my mind about my natural ability to comprehend the Bible. I confess:

"Lord, I am so slow to learn. Forgive me! Why is it, Lord, that I think I can understand your Word without your Holy Spirit? Open my eyes. Open my mind. Give me some good insights into your Word that I might share with your people so that they too will understand your Word and grow in their faith."

Though on the surface opening the Bible and determining to pray for enlightenment or to turn our hearts and minds toward God through praise seems rather simple, if not even mechanical, this is certainly not true. The devil, working with our natural human reason, wants us to rush into the Scriptures. Martin Luther spoke of that as coming to the Word of God as "pigs with dirty feet." The Holy Spirit himself has to continually remind us and teach us to depend upon him.

The Results

The results of praying for the enlightenment of the Holy Spirit are not immediate, which might leave the impression that such prayer is ineffective. But this is not the case at all. We patiently wait upon the Holy Spirit to quicken his Word. We might compare praying for the enlightenment of the Holy Spirit to turning up the thermostat on a cold day. The results are not instantaneous, but 15 minutes later the room is warmer.

In sermon preparation, after praying for enlightenment and expressing my dependency upon the Holy Spirit, I soon begin to receive some enlightened thoughts regarding my sermon text and the application.

This experience with the Bible is not only reserved for preachers. Every Christian who opens up the Bible to a meaningful text and expresses the desire to be enlightened by the Holy Spirit will experience this same dynamic of receiving enlightened thoughts and insights into the Word of God.

How to Pray

In approaching the Bible, I have found that brief, spontaneous prayers for enlightenment and expressions of praise and dependency upon God are the most effective. This is not a formal prayer—a kneel-down, fold-your-hands, bow-your-head prayer—but just a simple expression of the heart toward God. It is a conscious profession of dependency upon him: "Open my eyes, Lord! Holy Spirit, enlighten my understanding! I thank you for your Word. Feed me through it."

While there is great value in developing a disciplined prayer life by setting aside time each day to pray, very often in our daily activities the brief, spontaneous expressions of the heart are the most effective forms of prayer. Martin Luther wrote that a prayer must "come from the heart spontaneously, without any prepared or prescribed words. It must speak its own language according to the fervor of the heart."

I have also found particular hymn verses to be very effective prayers for enlightenment. For example:

> Renew me, O eternal Light, and let my heart and soul be bright, illumined with the light of grace that issues from your holy face.

Or in the words of one of Luther's hymns:

> Come, holy Light, guide divine, now cause the Word of life to shine. Teach us to know our God aright and call him Father with delight.

Before we can see wonderful things in the Word of God, we need to pray that the Holy Spirit will open our eyes and enlighten our minds. We do not pray in order to "bring the Spirit." It is the Holy Spirit himself who is urging us to direct our hearts and minds toward God.

There are times when seeking understanding of the Word of God through the enlightenment of the Holy Spirit might be a lengthy process. For example, I searched out the meaning of Galatians 2:20 for nearly six months. But don't lose heart, because God has promised that his Word will never return empty. It will always accomplish the purposes for which it was delivered (Isaiah 55:10,11).

What Does God Want Us to Know?

The Holy Spirit, prayer, and the Bible—these are the necessary ingredients to receive the enlightenment of the Holy Spirit, grasp God's truth, and be transformed. But the Bible is a very large book! What subject matter in the Bible should we focus upon as we pray for the enlightenment of the Holy Spirit?

First of all, let me assure you that my purpose in writing this book is not to promote biblical knowledge for the sake of gaining biblical knowledge. I am not interested in having you know certain biblical facts so that you might win at "Bible Trivia" or "Bible Baseball," nor am I attempting to turn you into theologians or trained interpreters of Scriptures. We seek the enlightenment of the Holy Spirit in order to gain specific, vital, life-changing knowledge that can come to us only through the pages of the Bible.

What is that knowledge?

In the first line of his massive work titled *The Institutes of the Christian Religion*, John Calvin writes: "Our wisdom, in so far as it ought to be deemed true and solid wisdom, consists almost entirely of two parts: the knowledge of God and of ourselves."[3]

We seek the enlightenment of the Holy Spirit and study the Bible in order to receive this twofold knowledge: *the knowledge of God and of ourselves.* But which should we seek first, the knowledge of God or the knowledge of ourselves?

If one were to write a formal, systematic, doctrinal treatment on the subjects of God and of man based upon the Bible, the teachings about God would come before the teachings about man. It would not be proper to first discuss the doctrine of man before discussing the doctrine of God. God, of course, comes first.

But if those teachings are to be applied to the human heart for the purpose of creating faith and producing transformation through preaching or through writing a book of this nature, the order must be reversed. Before seeking the enlightenment of the Holy Spirit and going to the Bible so that we might discover the life-changing grace of God as manifested in Christ Jesus, we must first seek to know what kind of people we are.

Therefore we first pray: "Holy Spirit, open our eyes. Enlighten our understanding so that we might know ourselves."

PRINCIPLE

Prayer does not "bring the Spirit,"
but as we seek the Lord through his Word,
prayer directs our hearts and minds
to the Holy Spirit.

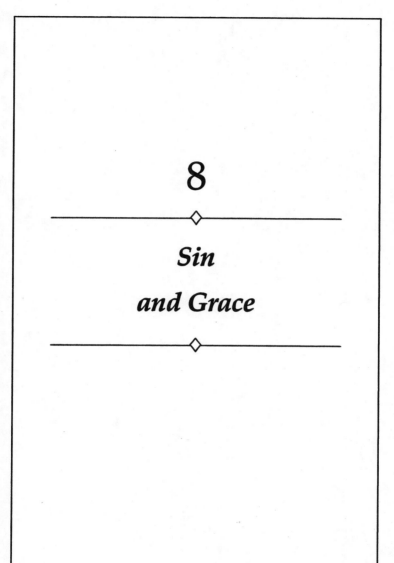

8

Sin and Grace

When we think of the word "enlightenment," positive thoughts come to mind.
An enlightened person is a smarter person, or, in some
ways, so to speak, a better person. He has been enlightened! He has acquired helpful knowledge and insights.

The eighteenth century is described as the "Age of
Enlightenment." Through the discovery of new truths
and scientific concepts, many of the archaic notions and
superstitions of the Middle Ages were rejected. The
world seemingly advanced. People became smarter. The
quality of life improved.

With that in mind, how would you respond to this
statement: "You need to have your eyes opened so that
you would know what a miserable, wretched sinner you

are"? Would you consider such enlightenment beneficial?

In the light of the new "enlightened" knowledge that comes out of modern psychology and teaches us to feel good about ourselves and to develop self-esteem, you would probably respond, "No thank you. I can do very well without that kind of enlightenment."

But...

What if such an eye-opening knowledge of your sin and the perversion of your human nature was a necessary prelude for pursuing an enlightened knowledge of God's life-changing love, grace, forgiveness, and power? Would you then be willing to see your sin in order to see the grace of God? Would you then be willing to uncover your weakness in order to touch the strength of God? Would you then be willing to turn away from yourself if such a turn brought you face-to-face with the Lord Jesus Christ and his love for you?

Seeing yourself through the eyes of God is "beneficial enlightenment." While such knowledge may be described as bad news, it is the necessary prelude for hearing and receiving *good news*. Without a knowledge of sin, we cannot understand what the Bible teaches about the grace and goodness of our God. Martin Luther wrote:

> If you want to engage profitably in the study of Holy Scripture and do not want to run head-on into a Scripture closed and sealed, then learn, above all things, to understand sin aright.[1]

Lukewarm Christians

Being confronted with the extent of our sin and seeking the life-changing grace of God is not a singular, once-for-all-time event that takes place at our conversion. "Sin and grace" is a process that is intended to occur throughout our Christian life and experience. The Bible tells us to "pursue" spiritual growth and sanctification, to be engaged in "fighting" the fight of faith, and, like new-born babes, to "crave" the pure milk of the Word of God. Such admonitions will fall on the deaf ears of those who do not acknowledge their sin and recognize their continual need for God's grace.

There are Christians who make the drastic mistake of thinking that once they are saved or converted they no longer need to examine their lives, uncover their sin, and seek God's grace. For this reason, the only testimony they have to offer is their conversion experience. They rehash the same experience over and over again. Since their initial conversion, their lives have remained virtually unchanged. Why? Because they no longer acknowledge the depth of their sin. They may say, *"I was once a sinner,* but now I have been saved!" What they don't realize is that they are still sinners and continually need to be saved from the negative consequences of their sin. While the issue of going to heaven was most certainly settled in their initial conversion, the quality of their daily living still falls short of the abundant, transformed life that Jesus promised.

In the book of Revelation, our Lord Jesus addressed and warned the various churches of that day. One of those churches, the church at Laodicea, was guilty of spiritual contentment. Jesus described their "lack of need" as being lukewarmness. In addressing this church Jesus minced no words: "You say, 'I am rich . . . and do not need a thing.' But you do not realize that you are wretched, pitiful, poor, blind and naked" (3:17). Obviously, the people to whom the Lord Jesus was addressing these words were Christians who thought of themselves more highly than they ought to think. They did not realize their sin.

Before we seek the eye-opening enlightenment of the Holy Spirit so that we might have our lives continually changed by the amazing grace of God, we must first seek the Holy Spirit to open our eyes to see ourselves as God sees us: "pitiful, poor, blind, and naked." David prayed, "Search me, O God, and know my heart; test me and know my anxious thoughts. See if there is any offensive way in me, and lead me in the way everlasting" (Psalm 139:23,24). As a result of seeing the depth of our sin, we will desire to touch the love, grace, mercy, and forgiveness of our God. Paul Tournier wrote:

> Believers who are the most desperate about themselves are the ones who express most forcefully their confidence in grace. . . . By degrees, the awareness of our guilt and of God's love increase side by side.[2]

The Battle over Sin

I realize that encouraging you to pray for the Holy Spirit to open your eyes to the depth of your sin and the perversion of your human nature is in opposition to the popular attitudes of the day. By nature we do not like the idea that we are sinners in need of the grace of God. We much prefer the message of some evangelical preachers who proclaim positive thinking, or the wisdom of the compassionate Christian counselors and psychologists who tell us to develop a sense of self-esteem and self-worth. Perhaps some of you have embraced the notion that regarding yourself as a "poor, miserable sinner" will do great damage to your sensitive human psyche. Rather than speaking about sin, you might prefer to apply other labels to your adverse attitudes and behavior which are not offensive to your human pride.

"I am not guilty of the sin of pride!" you might claim; "I am codependent."

"I am not filled with self-pity; I have a wounded heart."

"I am not self-centered; I have been injured by the events in my past."

"I am not an unforgiving person; I have been abused as a child."

"My alcoholism is not a lack of self-control; I am sick."

"My fears and worries are not the lack of faith; I am having an anxiety attack."

"My lack of joy and peace is not a sin; I am depressed."

What we do not realize is that these redefinitions are actually hurting us because we are not being encouraged to seek God's life-changing grace. We have been duped into thinking that the answer is found in uncovering the causes for our negative emotions and behavior. Rather than seeking God, we go to a counselor for self-understanding. Rather than confessing our sin, we acknowledge our self-worth in the face of the negative experiences of the past.

Now don't get me wrong: I am not so foolish as to deny the obvious psychological cause and effect that does exist in the development of human behavior. This is not the issue. Such causes and effects certainly exist. If I was rejected as a child, my life might very well manifest anger and resentment. *But this does not mean that such anger and resentment is justified because of the rejection.* It is still sin and must be confessed as such if I wish to touch the grace of God and be changed. In the case of serial killer Jeffrey Dahmer, there were certainly external causes that affected his behavior, but that doesn't make his behavior any less sinful.

Those who downplay the reality of human sin do not realize the destructive impact they are having upon the Christian Gospel. They are hindering the effective life-changing power of the grace of God. One well-known preacher explains his anti-sin attitude this way:

> I don't think that anything has been done in the name of Christ and under the banner of Christianity that has proven more destructive

to human personality, and hence counter-productive to the evangelistic enterprise, than the unchristian, uncouth strategy of attempting to make people aware of their lost and sinful condition.[3]

A professor at a leading evangelical seminary writes:

If our sin is viewed as causing the death of Jesus on the cross, then we ourselves become victims of a "psychological battering" produced by the cross. When I am led to feel that the pain and torment of Jesus' death is due to my sin, I inflict upon myself spiritual and psychological torment.[4]

How are we to regard such teachers? Are they friends or enemies of the Christian faith? Listen to the opinion of the great reformer John Calvin:

I am not unaware how much more plausible the view is, which invites us rather to ponder on our good qualities than to contemplate what must overwhelm us with shame—our miserable destitution and ignominy. There is nothing more acceptable to the human mind than flattery. . . . Whoever, therefore, gives heed to those teachers who merely employ us in contemplating our good qualities . . . will be plunged into the most pernicious ignorance.[5]

The astonishing thing is that those who stand against the teaching of human sin and guilt are also quick to suggest that the grace of God is an insufficient remedy for human ills. They believe that the theories of modern psychology must be appended to the Christian message in order to more effectively help hurting people.

For example, a popular book defining the principles involved in the integration of psychology and theology states:

> Many individual Christians look to psychology for new insights that will relieve personal discomfort or despair. They hope that psychology will provide answers to questions not specifically addressed in Christianity.[6]

Dr. Gary Collins writes in his book *Can You Trust Psychology?*

> Some human problems are not mentioned in Scripture. They are not discussed specifically, neither are there examples to show how others dealt with these issues in a way pleasing to God.[7]

This attitude is not hard to understand. The grace of God appears insufficient to them because they have downplayed the reality of human sin. It is a vicious circle. If you downplay sin, you cheapen grace.

There is a cause and effect which is far more vital and life-changing than the causes and effects uncovered by modern psychology. It is *the cause and effect that exists between confessing our sins and receiving God's grace.* That "cause and effect" has literally changed the lives of millions of people long before the study of psychology even existed.

We can only conclude that those who stand against the pervasive reality of human sin have not been deeply touched by the grace of God. If they knew the life-changing power of divine grace, they would desire to search out their lives and uncover every thought, word, action, or attitude that is contrary to God's will, recognize it as sin, repent, and seek God. And they would teach other people to do the same.

Human Weakness, Divine Strength

If we are willing to touch life-changing spiritual reality, we must see ourselves as God sees us: miserably weak sinners in need of grace. We will see our senseless reactions against the situations of life, our self-centeredness, our self-pity, our failure to rejoice in the Lord at all times, our hurt pride, our roller-coaster emotions, our desire for understanding and acceptance (rather than grace) as sins against God. As a result, we will seek God and desire the Holy Spirit to open our eyes to his truth so that we will be set free.

We make a terrible mistake when we cover over or give permission to our negative attitudes and emotions because we feel they are justified. "They are not sins," we think. "They are natural human responses and emotions." I have met many Christians who, in discussing with me their personal problems or conflicts, have asked the question, "Pastor, was what I did a sin?" They seek justification for their behavior because they do not realize the beneficial nature of acknowledging even their borderline attitudes and behavior as sin. As a result, they come short of experiencing the grace of God.

We need the Holy Spirit to open our eyes so that we might clearly see the degree to which sin pervades our lives. We do not seek the exposure of our sin in order to be "psychologically battered," but in order to have the Holy Spirit open our eyes to the life-changing grace of God in Christ Jesus.

This is not difficult to understand. A person who is not willing to face his sickness will not desire the services of a physician. If something isn't broken, you don't fix it. If you have no needs, you will have no desire to reach out for help. And if you don't know the brokenness of your human condition, you obviously do not require the provision that God offers.

Soren Kierkegaard pointed out that a person who is remote from his own guilt and failure is also remote from God, because he is remote from himself.[8]

The Bible is very clear in revealing to us the divine estimate of human nature. Being born out of the root of Adam, we are the children of wrath (Ephesians 2:3), totally unable by nature to grasp the things of the Spirit of God (1 Corinthians 2:14). The Bible tells us that we were shaped in iniquity and born in sin (Psalm 51:5) and that the imaginations of our hearts are evil (Genesis 8:21). Within our human flesh there dwells absolutely no good thing. Even though we may desire to do good and to be good, we are unable to accomplish our lofty ideals because our nature is wrong (Romans 7:18,19). We are in bondage to the law of sin and death (Romans 7:21-23).

Putting it very simply, from God's point of view our lives are a mess! We need self-accusation, not self-esteem. We need grace, not acceptance and understanding. We need to be rescued from ourselves, not supported by a group of fellow sinners.

The Beginning of Spiritual Progress

If you read of the experiences of other Christians who progressed in their knowledge of God's life-changing grace, you will note this combination of a deep sense of sin and failure together with a deep appreciation for God. Men the likes of Paul the apostle, John Calvin, and Martin Luther were not afraid to speak of their sinful nature and even boast of their weaknesses, because they knew of the grace of God. The writings of such men reflect a profound level of spiritual depth and insight.

For example, Martin Luther's discovery of the great doctrine of justification by grace was not an isolated incident. There was a great struggle with sin and guilt that took place leading up to the day when his eyes were opened and he was able to clearly understand that God had actually declared him to be righteous through Jesus Christ. It was his very keen sense of sin and failure that was the driving force behind his discovery. In fact, he stated that it was when he was at the point of deepest despair over his sin that he was actually the closest to grace.[9]

The reformer John Calvin was referred to by his friends as "the accusative case" because he had a profound sense of his own sin.

Don't be afraid to confront yourself head-on and thereby uncover your sinful condition. Your pride may argue against what the Holy Spirit is trying to show you. You may struggle and squirm when he turns on the light and exposes your thoughts, attitudes, self-centeredness, priorities, and ambitions. Stripped of every pretense of righteousness, you will stand before God seeing yourself as he sees you. This is the real you, prepared to be touched by the transforming grace of God.

Therefore we pray, "Search me, O God!"

PRINCIPLE

*Personal dissatisfaction and self-accusation
are the prelude for the Holy Spirit
to open our eyes to the truth
of the Gospel of Jesus Christ.*

9

◇

The Life-Changing
Power of Grace

◇

O ur Father in heaven does not show us our hearts, open our eyes to our faults, and bring us to a place of guilt and condemnation in order to forsake us. God does not turn his back on us in our time of need. He desires to reveal himself to us as a God of love, mercy, and forgiveness. He wants to change and transform our lives by his grace, and for this very purpose he has given to us his Son Jesus Christ.

The compassion of God for sinful humanity is revealed in Christ. The writer to the Hebrews declares: "In the past God spoke to our forefathers through the prophets at many times and in various ways, but in these last days he has spoken to us by his Son. . . . The Son is the radiance of God's glory and the exact representation of his being" (Hebrews 1:1-3). In response to his disciples, who asked him to show them the Father, Jesus clearly stated, "If you have seen me, you have seen the Father." When we look at Jesus as he is revealed to us in the four Gospels, we see the desires and purposes of our God.

For example, in the attitude of Jesus toward sinners— his willingness to reach out to the sick, the needy, and the downtrodden—we discover that our God is concerned about our needs. Jesus expressed the desire of his Father in heaven when he said, "Come to me, all you who are weary and burdened, and I will give you rest" (Matthew 11:28). As he walked upon this earth, Jesus Christ was most certainly a sufficient solution for all human ills.

What About Us, Today?

It is not difficult for us to understand how Jesus reached out to hurting people as he walked upon this earth and changed their lives. He was there for them. He could directly touch their lives. But what about us today? What about our hurts and fears, our anxiety and emotional distress? Does Jesus offer to us today the same help and compassion as he did to the people of his day? If so, *how does his compassion extend to us today?*

I am sure there are hurting people who wish that Jesus could come back and touch their lives today, but according to the apostle Paul, for us to be changed by the saving power of Jesus Christ, it is not necessary for Jesus to be among us in the flesh. Paul explains how Jesus touches our lives today in Romans 10:6-8:

> Do not say in your heart, "Who will ascend into heaven?" (that is, to bring Christ down) or, "Who will descend into the deep?" (that is, to bring Christ up from the dead). But what does it say? "The word is near you; it is in your

mouth and in your heart," that is, the word of
faith we are proclaiming.

According to the apostle Paul, the life-changing power
and grace of God are delivered to us through the Word of
God. Having Jesus touch our lives through his Word
rather than as a result of his earthly presence is not an
inferior method. In fact, Jesus himself told his disciples
that it was *better* for them that he was going away,
because the Holy Spirit, whom he described as "the
Comforter," would be given to them. By attaching himself to the Word of God, the Holy Spirit would convict
hearts and change lives (John 16:7,8).

The Gospel of Jesus Christ

It is in the death and resurrection of Jesus Christ that
God clearly reveals the extent of his compassion for us.
Nearly 2000 years ago, in the city of Jerusalem, Jesus
Christ died on the cross. He bore our sins, our failures,
our grief and shame, our worry and anxiety, our pride
and self-centeredness in his own body and suffered the
due penalty for these our sins. To demonstrate that the
victory had been gained for us, God raised Jesus from
the dead.

As the result of those saving events, God declares us
to be forgiven. He has given to us the perfect righteousness of his Son Jesus. God reveals his power and love by
showering upon us his grace. Regarding the benefits of
Jesus' death on the cross, the apostle Paul writes: "In him
we have redemption through his blood, the forgiveness
of sins, in accordance with the riches of God's grace that
he lavished on us with all wisdom and understanding"
(Ephesians 1:7,8).

Because Jesus died on the cross and rose again, God
lavishes upon us his grace, and *that grace is there for us.*
Initiated by the power of the forgiveness of sins, God

works in us a new life here on earth filled with joy and peace, and the living hope of an eternal life in heaven. He gives us all of these benefits solely on account of the death and resurrection of our Lord Jesus Christ. The apostle Paul writes, "Praise be to the God and Father of our Lord Jesus Christ, who has blessed us in the heavenly realms with every spiritual blessing in Christ" (Ephesians 1:3). The apostle Peter put it this way: "His divine power has given us everything we need for life and godliness through our knowledge of him" (2 Peter 1:3).

The meaning, significance, and life-changing power of the death and resurrection of Jesus Christ was revealed to the apostles and prophets by the Holy Spirit. This revelation of the Spirit became the substance of the Christian proclamation and is called *the Gospel of Jesus Christ*. The apostle Paul writes, "We preach Christ crucified: a stumbling block to Jews and foolishness to Gentiles, but to those whom God has called, both Jews and Greeks, Christ the power of God and the wisdom of God" (1 Corinthians 1:23,24).

The Gospel is a promise from God to forgive us. The gracious forgiveness of sins offered in the Gospel is life-changing. In describing the effect of the Gospel, Paul writes, "I am not ashamed of the gospel, for it is the power of God for the salvation of everyone who believes" (Romans 1:16).

The meaning of the word "salvation" does not involve only eternal life in heaven, as some have interpreted it. It also involves deliverance from the consequences of our earthly problems and conflicts today. God does not only promise us eternal life in heaven, but he has also promised us an abundant life on earth.

The Power of the Gospel to Produce Change

When we bring our sins to the cross of Jesus Christ and receive the promise of forgiveness offered in the

Gospel, something happens to us. Our lives are deeply affected.

For example, being from New York City, where the flow of life is quite hectic, I became accustomed to moving with a rapid flow of traffic, hitting the accelerator just as the light turns green and quickly taking my right-of-way at a four-way stop sign or green arrow. Moving to the Midwest exposed me to a totally different mentality. As a result, I would readily "blow my cool" when I was in a hurry and boxed in by a herd of snails.

I know that Jesus tells me in the Sermon on the Mount not to react to situations of life. Of all the teachings of Jesus, I have the greatest difficulty with his nonreactionary stance. Reacting against those who hurt us or speak unkind things about us is the way life is lived. We are all reactionary people. We are programmed to believe that we have the right to defend ourselves, stand up for ourselves, not take any guff from anybody, and preserve our space. Getting upset by those who unnecessarily cause us delay is the *normal* thing to do.

One day in a senseless traffic jam, after I blew off some steam, my eyes were opened to the truth that my reaction was a sin against God. As a result, I acknowledged it as sin, told the Lord I was sorry, brought my sin to the cross, and received by faith the forgiveness that the Gospel of Jesus Christ offers.

As I acknowledged that Jesus was willing to put up with evildoers and shed his blood on the cross so that my sins, including my sin of reaction, would be forgiven, I felt very small and foolish. The Holy Spirit impressed upon me that while Jesus was willing to submit to death for me, I was not willing to put up with even the slightest adversity.

As the result of acknowledging the sin of my negative reactions, bringing it to the cross of Jesus Christ, and receiving my forgiveness, something in my heart was changed by God's wonderful grace.

I challenge you to do the same thing with your worry, fear, and anxiety, your pride and desire for self-esteem, your self-centeredness and self-pity, your anger, bitterness, and depression, your broken relationships and failure to forgive, your negative reactions to the adversities of life, your pettiness and easily hurt pride, and your failure to rejoice in the Lord always. Acknowledge these things as sin. Bring them to the cross of Jesus Christ. Receive your forgiveness—*and see what happens.*

In Luke 13 our Lord Jesus laments over the conditions that existed in the city of Jerusalem. He reveals to us his heart. He desired to embrace his people and gather them under his wings as a hen gathers her chicks. *But the people were not willing.*

I think our Lord Jesus also laments over the conditions that exist in the lives of his children today. Like the people of his day, so many Christians are not willing to acknowledge their sin and their need of grace, and come to the Lord Jesus so that he might embrace them under his cross and say to them, "Be of good cheer. Your sins are forgiven."

PRINCIPLE

*When we acknowledge our sin,
bring that sin to the cross of Jesus Christ,
and receive his forgiveness,
something happens to us.
We are changed!*

10

◇

The Mysterious

Gospel

◇

*T*he Gospel, which offers to us the forgiveness of sins, life and salvation in Jesus Christ,
is the essence of Christianity. It is the instrument of the
Holy Spirit. If we want to experience the life-changing
power of God, we have to clearly understand and receive
by faith the dynamic promises of the Gospel. That message has to infect our minds and be burned into our
hearts. The Gospel is the means by which God delivers
to us his life-changing grace.

My purpose is not to present to you all the aspects and
nuances of the Gospel of Jesus Christ, which include the
forgiveness of sins, justification, sanctification, reconciliation, atonement, redemption, the mystical union of
Christ dwelling within us, the second coming of Jesus,

etc. To do so would demand the writing of many volumes. My purpose is to motivate you to discover the Gospel for yourself by getting into the Word of God and seeking the enlightenment of the Holy Spirit.

The Gospel, as distinguished from the Law, is always a word of promise. It tells us *what God has done for us*. John Calvin writes, "By the Gospel, I understand the clear manifestation of the mystery of Christ. . . . It includes all the promises by which God reconciles men to himself."[1] Martin Luther defines the Gospel as a "preaching and proclamation of the grace and mercy of God through Jesus Christ, merited and won by his death."[2]

The Gospel of Jesus Christ is a mystery. We are not able to beneficially grasp the meaning and significance of the death and resurrection of Jesus Christ through our natural reason and intelligence. The Gospel is not human wisdom; it is divine wisdom. The apostle Paul describes God's plan for reaching out to sinful mankind through the death and resurrection of his Son Jesus Christ as "secret wisdom" which can only be revealed by the Spirit (1 Corinthians 2:7-10). In fact, according to natural human reason, the wisdom of God revealed in the Gospel is foolishness. Only by the enlightenment of the Holy Spirit can we understand what God has accomplished for us in Christ Jesus.

Ignorance of the Gospel

Even though this message of the Gospel is the essence of Christianity and is revealed in the Bible, many Christians do not have a clear understanding of the Gospel. They may acknowledge the historical reality of the death of Jesus Christ on the cross, but their eyes are closed as to how that message applies to them. Their hearts have not been touched and their lives affected. For this reason they come short of experiencing God's life-changing power.

In one of the congregations where I was the pastor I was accused by a group of people, some of whom were "leading members" of the congregation, of "not preaching the Gospel." While they were certain that "preaching the Gospel" was a very important ingredient in the Sunday morning service (which was to their credit), somehow they were confused as to what the Gospel actually was. They felt that I was not preaching it, and this greatly concerned me, since I knew that I preached the Gospel of Jesus Christ every Sunday. They called for a special meeting of the congregation to consider their concern.

After much discussion it became clear that my critics were confused over the definition of the word "Gospel." What they meant was that I was not preaching "from the Gospels." In our denomination we follow the appointed Scripture lessons for the year. There are three Bible lessons every Sunday: one from the Old Testament, one from the epistles, and a third from one of the four Gospels. That particular year I had determined to preach from the appointed epistle lessons rather than from the Old Testament or Gospel lessons. I announced this in the beginning of the Advent season. According to their understanding, I was not "preaching the Gospel" because I was not preaching "from the Gospels."

They did not understand the meaning of a word which they had heard over and over again. They did not realize that there was a difference between the "four Gospels," which refer to the biblical books of Matthew, Mark, Luke, and John, and the message of the "Gospel," which offers the promise of forgiveness of sins, life, and eternal salvation through the death and resurrection of Jesus Christ. Even though I was using texts from the epistles as the basis for my Sunday sermon, I was still preaching the Gospel of Jesus Christ.

This example of confusion is not an isolated incident. In my own denomination, for example, a survey was conducted some years ago. One of the questions asked was, "What is the main emphasis of the Gospel?" Fifty-nine percent of those questioned stated that they believed that the main emphasis of the Gospel was upon God's rules for right living.

The Gospel has absolutely nothing to do with "rules for right living." It is just the opposite. It is a powerful, life-changing message of what God has done for us in Christ Jesus. It is not a directive to live a good life, but is a promise from God that offers the forgiveness of sins, life, and salvation.

The essence of Christianity is the Gospel. While the Bible speaks about many subjects and provides many facts of history as well as many religious rules and regulations, the life-changing heart and core of the Bible is the Gospel of Jesus Christ. We read and study the Bible in order to learn about Jesus and hear the good news of what he has done for us.

Confusion

Failure to understand the Gospel results in great confusion over the nature and teachings of Christianity. As a Christian pastor for over 25 years I have had countless opportunities to speak with people about Christianity. I have often been amazed by their gross misconceptions. It is a rare treat to find a person who truly understands what it means to be Christian.

For example, at the request of some members of my congregation I conducted a funeral for a family with whom I was not acquainted. I sat down with the niece of the deceased, who claimed to be a Christian, in order to get some information.

"Was your uncle a Christian?" I gently inquired.

"Of course he was," she firmly responded. "He was a very good man. He lived a good life. Everybody liked him."

Without seeming to appear too pushy, I continued the questioning. "Well, that's great," I responded. "It's nice to know that he was such a good man, but was he a Christian?"

"He seldom went to church, if that's what you mean," she responded, becoming a little disturbed. "I think he had a Bible, but I don't know if he ever read it."

"Being a Christian," I began to explain, "is more than going to church or owning a Bible. Christians believe that their sins are forgiven and that they have eternal life because of the death and resurrection of Jesus Christ. Did your uncle believe in Jesus?"

"Oh," she replied, obviously embarrassed. "I don't know anything about that!"

This confusion is widespread. If you don't believe me, try asking some of the people with whom you work or interact daily what it means to be a Christian. See what kind of answers you get. You might be very surprised. While of course a very few would correctly define Christianity by the Gospel, others would focus on the Ten Commandments or would appeal to church membership and involvement. Still others would identify a Christian by love, or by "the Golden Rule," or by involvement in religious rites or traditions. I knew one man who identified a Christian as someone who was not a Jew. Even though we claim to be a Christian nation, only a very small percentage of alleged "Christian" people actually know what it means to be a Christian.

This same ignorance does not exist among people who embrace other world religions, such as Islam or Hinduism, because it is not difficult to understand or explain a religion which is based upon laws, rules or religious rituals. Relating to God by way of rules, regulations, and rituals fits our natural way of thinking. It is easily understood. Martin Luther wrote that "the Gospel is a sort of teaching which cannot, like the teaching of the Law, be understood by reason, but with which reason utterly disagrees."[3]

On a recent trip to the Middle East, we visited Egypt. Our guide in Egypt was a Muslim. One of the members of our group asked him what Muslims believed. He clearly, precisely, and in an orderly fashion explained the principles of Islam. His explanation was very easy to understand. Muslims believe that there is one god, and Mohammed is his prophet. They pray. They fast. They give to the poor. And they take a trip to the city of Mecca. Basically, that's what it means to be a Muslim.

While a religion of rules, regulations, and rituals is very logical, it is not logical that the grace and forgiveness of God is given to us through the death and resurrection of Jesus Christ. The Gospel is supernatural truth. Without the enlightenment of the Holy Spirit, the Gospel can not be beneficially grasped, and if the Gospel is not grasped, *our lives will not be affected.*

Why is it that there are so many Christians today who seek secular solutions for their human problems? The answer is very simple: *They have not beneficially grasped the good news of the Gospel of Jesus Christ. Their eyes remain closed and their hearts unaffected.*

PRINCIPLE

*God uses the message
of the death and resurrection of Jesus Christ
as the instrument to produce change
within our lives.*

11

The Miracle
of Faith

The apostle Paul focuses his primary attention upon the Gospel of Jesus Christ. He refers to the preaching of the cross of Christ as a stumbling block to the Jews and foolishness to the Greeks. The Gospel is "God's secret wisdom, a wisdom that has been hidden." This message, according to the apostle, has been revealed to us by the Spirit of God, and it is only through the Holy Spirit that we are able to comprehend it. As Paul writes, "The man without the Spirit does not accept the things that come from the Spirit of God, for they are foolishness to him, and he cannot understand them" (1 Corinthians 2:7,10,14).

Rather than believing the Gospel, it is far more reasonable to believe that we are pleasing God and therefore going to heaven because of our good works. This is pure human logic. It fits into our natural way of thinking. Every world religion with the exception of Christianity maintains such a posture.

It is also far more reasonable to seek the help of counselors and psychologists rather than to believe that God is able to change our lives through a message about Jesus Christ. To believe that the death and resurrection of a Jewish Rabbi in the city of Jerusalem nearly 2000 years ago will forgive our sins, remove our guilt, deal with our fear, take away our worry, settle our emotions, provide us peace, and give us an eternal hope is not reasonable. To the natural mind it is foolishness. Therefore, without the enlightenment of the Holy Spirit, we can neither understand nor believe the Gospel.

Focusing on the Gospel

If the Gospel of Jesus Christ were the only possession of the Christian church, it would not be difficult to identify Christianity by the Gospel. But this is not the case. Focusing upon human behavior, social issues, and good works are also a part of the teachings of Christianity drawn from the Bible. It is therefore not strange that people say, "I am going to heaven because I have obeyed the Ten Commandments." It is not strange that some have seen Christianity and psychology as being compatible. After all, do they not both deal with human behavior?

In addition, over the years we have added to the Gospel much paraphernalia in the way of our own traditions, church rules and regulations, spiritual experiences, gimmicks, and worship rituals so that the message of the Gospel always seems to get lost in the shuffle.

For this reason the Christian church for the past 2000 years has been continually discovering and rediscovering the Gospel. With all the confusion today over the integration of psychology and theology, with the intrusion into the church of Recovery Programs and support groups, with emphasis upon Church Growth and Signs and Wonders, never has there been a time more ripe for the rediscovery of the powerful, life-changing Gospel of Jesus Christ.

Isolating the Gospel

In order to understand the centrality of the Gospel of Jesus Christ, it would be good for us to go back to the very beginning, to the first century of the Christian era, and try to put ourselves into the place of those who heard "the strange message" for the first time. If we do this, we will soon recognize that the message of the Gospel of Jesus Christ is the heart and core of Christianity and is the means which God employs to transform our lives.

After Jesus ascended into heaven, the apostles preached about the meaning of his death and resurrection. The apostle Paul took the message of the Gospel to the Gentiles. The Holy Spirit worked through his words, and thousands were converted to Christianity. They believed in Jesus. Their sins were forgiven. They were filled with the Holy Spirit, and the church rapidly grew.

There were no traditions, rules, rituals, and practices among the first-century Gentile Christians to overshadow the message of the Gospel. While the Jewish converts still had to deal with their traditions and rituals (such as circumscision, which often got in the way of the Gospel), the Gentiles heard a message with no strings attached. Those who believed in Jesus Christ did so as the sole result of the miracle of the Holy Spirit opening their eyes and producing faith.

If you put yourself into the place of a first-century Gentile who is confronted for the first time with the message of the Gospel of Jesus Christ, you will better understand what is meant by the "miracle of enlightenment and faith."

"I Believe It!"

One morning you decide to go to town to do some shopping. When you arrive at the town square, you see a commotion taking place. A man is standing in the midst of the square, proclaiming some message to about 30 or 40 people who seem quite interested. Out of curiosity, you draw closer to the group.

". . . and God determined that this Jesus of Nazareth should be put to death by the Romans," the speaker proclaims. "God put all of your sins upon him. He suffered the penalty for the things that you have done wrong. On the third day after his death, God raised him from the dead. Believing in him, you have the forgiveness of all of your sins and eternal life with God."

You had never heard this strange teaching before, but as the man continues to preach and explain this message about Jesus of Nazareth, *a very mysterious thing happens to you*: You begin to believe the message! Your eyes are opened. You clearly understand what the man is talking about. While you have "spiritual needs" and perhaps are plagued by a sense of guilt which is not removed by appeasing your pagan gods, you have no reason whatsoever to believe that this message is true. Yet something inside you is telling you that what he is saying is true and that the message is for you. Your eyes have been opened!

You actually understand the message and believe it! You believe that Jesus died for your sins. You claim the forgiveness of your sins. You believe that you have eternal life. You believe it! Joy begins to well up within your heart. You know that your God loves you.

But the problem is that not everyone believes it. Some scoff and laugh at the speaker. But there are others, like yourself, who believe the message.

After the speaker finishes and the crowd begins to disperse, there is a small group of you who remain. You gather closely around the speaker. "What is next?" you ask him. "What are we supposed to do now?"

The speaker explains to you about being baptized and forming a church fellowship. So you, together with your fellow converts, are baptized and make plans to regularly gather, break bread together, and share your new-found relationship with Jesus Christ.

"You Believe What?"

Can you imagine the response of your friends and relatives to your announcement that you have embraced a new "religion"? After trying to explain the basics of your newfound faith to your husband or wife, the response might possibly be something like this:

"Now explain that to me again," your spouse asks. "You're telling me that you believe that a Jewish Rabbi by the name of Jesus was executed by the Romans and was raised from the dead. Because of his death and resurrection, you believe that your sins are forgiven and you have eternal life. This is why you have such joy, peace, and contentment? Is that about it, dear? Are you sure you're feeling okay?"

But while you are living in the midst of many scoffers and unbelievers, even within your own family, your faith remains strong. You regularly gather together with your fellow Christians and talk about Jesus and share his Supper. You long to hear the Gospel message over and over again because through it your life was changed. Jesus is your Lord! He is your Savior! Through the Gospel your eyes were opened, your heart was warmed, you believed the message, and changes began to take place in your life.

You Receive A Letter . . .

One day your little fellowship receives a letter from the man who first came to your town and preached the Gospel. He is explaining to you in greater detail the teachings about Jesus Christ, addressing some of the problems that may arise in your fellowship, and encouraging you to stand firm in your faith. This letter becomes very precious because it produces in your heart the same effect that was produced when you heard the Gospel for the first time. The letter is faith-productive. Again, your heart is touched.

You make handwritten copies of your letter and pass them on to other fellowships in nearby towns and cities. You also receive the benefit of reading the letters that were written to them. The letters are saved and read over and over again. They are precious because they produce results in the hearts of people. The leaders in your fellowship use the content of these letters as the basis for their teaching and preaching.

Now then, in conclusion, how would you answer this question: "How does God work in order to create faith and transform human lives?"

The answer is obvious: He works through the message of the Gospel of Jesus Christ. Because you heard the Gospel of Jesus Christ, for some mysterious reason your heart was warmed, your eyes were opened and you believed it! As a result, you would never be the same again.

Maintaining the Purity of the Gospel

Imagine, if you will, a group of first-century "counselors and psychologists" offering a proposition to the apostle Paul. "We are concerned by human behavior as you also are concerned," they say, "and we have developed various theories and notions as to why people do what they do. We would like to integrate our ideas on human behavior with your message. What do you think?"

How do you think the apostle would have responded? I think he would have told them very clearly that, while their concern for human behavior was admirable, their notions could not be mixed with what the Holy Spirit had revealed to him about the death and resurrection of Jesus Christ. The apostle Paul was living in an age in which Greek philosophy was flourishing. The Gnostics were a group of alleged Christians who attempted to mix the Christian Gospel with pagan notions. Especially in his letter to the Colossians, Paul made it very clear that the message of the Gospel must remain pure and unadulterated.

Today in the church, even though the way in which God tranforms lives has not changed, there are many Christian leaders who welcome the integration of secular concepts developed by unbelievers into the Christian proclamation. In fact, there are even Christian teachers and preachers who are willing to adjust or redefine the message of the Gospel in order to make room for secular concepts.

This distortion of the Christian Gospel undermines the very essence of Christianity and leads to confusion in the minds of people. The essence of Christianity is found in *the Gospel of Jesus Christ*, not in the understanding of human behavior.

We must be willing to fight to maintain the purity of the Gospel. The message of human sin and divine grace is not irrelevant. Yet those who are seeking to integrate psychological theories into Christianity are causing it to become irrelevant. There is nothing lacking in the Gospel of Jesus Christ. It transformed lives in the first century and will produce the same results today.

PRINCIPLE

*As the Holy Spirit opens our eyes
and produces faith through the hearing
of the Gospel, our lives are transformed.
This is an ongoing process.
We hear the same message over and over again.
Why? Because we sin over and over again!*

12

◇

God Gives,

Faith Receives

◇

*T*he same confusion that exists today over the essence of Christianity due to a lack of understanding of the Gospel also existed at the time of the Reformation. Since Protestants were coming out of the religion of Rome and were totally unfamiliar with the teachings of the Bible, they lacked clear teaching. For this reason, it was necessary for Martin Luther to precisely define what Christianity was all about. Read carefully what he wrote:

> One is a Christian, not because he gives to Christ but because he accepts from Christ. A Christian is not an active but a passive person, one who only allows things to be given to him.

*If you do not permit things to be given to you, you are
no Christian.*[1]

This definition, like everything else associated with
the Gospel, runs contrary to the natural process of religious thinking. While being a receiver or a taker is not
the basis for our relationships with one another, *it is the
basis for our relationship with God.* Christians are not
"doers for God" but "receivers from God." They are not
active workers, but are first and foremost *passive receivers.*
They are people whose eyes have been opened to the
meaning of the death and resurrection of the Lord Jesus
and whose hands receive God's great and many blessings. To be a Christian, we do not do something, nor do
we join something. To be a Christian, we receive by faith
the blessings of forgiveness of sins, life, and salvation
offered to us in the death and resurrection of our Lord
Jesus Christ.

"I Thought We Were 'Do-Gooders' "

I realize that some people might be a little disturbed by
this definition. Usually Christians have been thought of
as "do-gooders" and "givers" of themselves for God and
for others. While "doing good" and being a "giver" is
most certainly one of the *results* of being a Christian, it is
not what *makes* a person a Christian. A person *becomes* a
Christian by first becoming a receiver of God's grace.

Thinking that a Christian is a Christian because he is
kind, loving, and considerate toward other people
implies that anyone who is such a "giving" person must
therefore be a Christian. Back in 1948, in the midst of the
Arab and Israeli conflict, one high-ranking U.S. Govern-
ment official allegedly said, "If these Arabs and Jews
would sit down around a bargaining table and act like
good Christians we would not have all this difficulty."

Defining "good Christians" as those willing to give to
each other and settle their conflicts in a kind and loving

manner is a very common misconception. A Christian is a kind, loving, and considerate person *because* he is a Christian. First he *becomes* a Christian, a "receiver of God's life-changing love and kindness," and as a result he offers the same love and kindness toward others.

In a popular folk song we sing, "They'll know we are Christians by our love." While this sounds good, it can easily leave the impression that a Christian is a Christian because of his love for others. Yet I know a woman who works in a counseling center in a major university who says of the counselors and psychologists working with her, "These are some of the kindest, most loving people I have ever met, yet they are all atheists." Obviously, even though they appear to be kind and loving people, if they do not believe the message of the Gospel of Jesus Christ, they are not Christians. Christians love *because they have been receivers of God's love for them.* This is the only kind of love that matters to God. We love *because* we have been loved.

Difficult to Receive

Being a passive receiver of God's grace is not easy! Human pride fights against the notion of being a taker. We believe that we will be thought of far more highly in this world if we are givers. So we try to work out our own problems and solve our own conflicts. We embrace the erroneous notion that "God helps those who help themselves." We would prefer self-help rather than divine help. But in fact when we deal with eternal life, we are helpless. As Christians we believe that Jesus died for the sole reason of getting us to heaven, but when offered the grace of God to deal with present life-related issues, we sometimes respond, "No thanks, I can help myself." It is not easy being a receiver of grace!

Ellen was a woman in one of my congregations who was always the first to help out in time of need. If someone was sick or if a family was bereaved, Ellen was always there, lending support, preparing food, or providing transportation. Because of her good deeds she was often spoken of as being "such a good Christian."

One day Ellen became sick and shut-in herself. The amazing thing is that she absolutely refused to receive any help from the other members of the congregation or anyone else, including her own family. Her pride was at stake. She was a "giver" and not a "receiver."

The problem is that if this same attitude of refusing to receive was reflected in Ellen's relationship with her God, she missed out on many of the blessings that God offered to her in Christ Jesus. In order to do the kind of giving that is pleasing to God, we must first be receivers from God.

What Is Faith?

Speaking of a Christian as being a "receiver" defines the nature and action of Christian faith. We all know that Christians are supposed to have faith. The Holy Spirit creates faith in our hearts through the hearing of the Gospel (Romans 10:17). But what is faith? How do we define faith? How does faith work?

Some believe that faith itself has the power to change our lives. They teach that when faith becomes joined to positive confession or visualization it produces positive results. They believe that we should have "faith in our own faith."

This is a major deception being taught in the church today. The truth is that it is *the Gospel of Jesus Christ* that produces results. Our faith itself is not productive! Our focus should be explicitly directed at what God has done in Christ Jesus, not at our own faith.

Others would simply say that faith is nothing more than believing or acknowledging that certain things are true even though they can neither be seen nor abstractly

proven. We "believe" in God even though we can neither see him nor prove his existence, but this is not the
essence of Christian faith. The Bible tells us that the devil
also believes that God exists.

While knowing, believing, and confessing are associated with faith, the real action of Christian faith is
trusting or grasping. Faith is the hand that reaches out and
grasps the promises of God. Another word that was
often used by the Reformers to define Holy Spirit-
produced faith is "appropriation." Faith "appropriates"
or "seizes" the promises of God. Martin Luther writes
that "only faith apprehends the promise, believes the
assurance God gives, and extends the hand to accept
what God is offering."[2] John Calvin clearly defines faith:

> Hence, in order that the Word of God may gain
> full credit, the mind must be enlightened and
> the heart confirmed from some other quarter.
> We shall now have a full definition of faith if
> we say that it is a firm and sure knowledge of
> the divine favor toward us, founded on the
> truth of a free promise in Christ, and sealed on
> our hearts by the Holy Spirit.[3]

Faith and promise are intimately related. What God
has promised faith grasps and appropriates. Where
there is faith, there first has to be a genuine promise.
Where God has granted benefits, faith is the hand that
grasps or appropriates those benefits. If you have faith,
you are a receiver of God's many blessings.

Think of it this way.

When Jesus died on the cross and rose again, God
granted to us many benefits. In a sense, we can speak of
these benefits as spiritual wealth deposited by God in a
checking account with our name on it. When we became
Christians, we were given our checkbook. God also provided us with the Bible which tells us what is available in

that account. In this analogy, the action of faith is to write checks and draw off the account.

Of course, if a person lives and dies and never writes a check, he never appropriates any of the benefits. What a tragedy! He was a spiritual millionaire but lived and died a spiritual pauper!

Unclaimed Wealth

The Gospel of Jesus Christ promises and offers to us the forgiveness of our sins, peace, joy, contentment, and eternal life in heaven. The failure to understand and believe the Gospel, in addition to creating confusion over the definition of Christianity, causes us to lose out on the promised benefits. This is very serious. Our eternal life in heaven is at stake. Our abundant life on earth will be lacking.

As a parish pastor, I can recall many sad incidents in which faithful church members missed the benefits of the death and resurrection of Jesus Christ because they did not know what God had promised. They were still in the dark. Their eyes were closed to what God had done for them. As a result, they were suffering, plagued by their sin and guilt. The prophet Hosea, referring to the people of his day, declared, "My people are destroyed from lack of knowledge" (4:6).

The Gift of Eternal Life

I was visiting one afternoon with an elderly gentleman. He was about 85 years old and growing weaker each day. He knew that he was going to die soon. He was a man who had been a member of a Christian congregation all his life. He had served on various boards and committees and faithfully supported the work of the church.

After we prayed together, he said to me, "Pastor, I'm scared to die. I don't know whether or not I'm going to heaven. I don't know if I have done enough to get to heaven. I have so many doubts."

After going to church for so many years, somehow he did not know that eternal life was a gift from God. Even though God had provided for his eternal life through the death and resurrection of the Lord Jesus, he was still trying to work his way into heaven. As a result he was suffering from fear and uncertainty. I shared with him the good news that a major benefit of the death of Jesus Christ was the gift of eternal life in heaven.

Would it not be a terrible tragedy if this man, a church member all his life, had missed the benefit of eternal life in heaven? Of course it is not possible to make such a judgment because we are not able to examine the heart to determine whether or not faith is really present. But the man's confession of fear and doubt was a cause for deep concern. On the basis of his own confession, his eternal salvation was in jeopardy. The issue had not been settled.

Fully Forgiven

One morning I had an appointment with a woman in her early twenties. She happened to be one of our Sunday school teachers. She told me that in her late teens she had had an abortion. She said, "I don't believe that God can or will forgive me for what I have done. I dream about this little five-year-old child that could have been mine. I have so much guilt. God could never forgive me."

She could not receive the assurance of the forgiveness of her sins because she did not understand the significance of the shedding of the blood of Jesus Christ on the cross. She did not know that Jesus had already suffered the ultimate punishment for her sins, including the sin which was plaguing her conscience. There are no sins that are not able to be completely covered and forgiven through the blood of Jesus Christ. As a result of her lack of understanding of the significance of the shed blood of Christ, she was suffering from severe guilt and condemnation.

Due to the present legality of abortion, we are living in an age in which the phenomenon called Post-Abortion Syndrome, characterized by a severe sense of guilt and shame, is becoming very prevalent. While our sinful attitude of vindictiveness might respond by saying, "It serves them right," as Christians whose lives have been touched by the grace and forgiveness of God, we must be prepared to offer that same grace and speak that same Gospel which assured us of our own forgiveness to those suffering from guilt and shame, regardless of the nature of their sin.

The Righteousness of Christ

One Sunday in Bible class I was teaching on the subject of justification by faith. One of the class members said, "Of course we all sin, but the key is, are we trying to be good? All God can expect of us is a sincere effort to do his will. As long as we try to do the best we can, God will understand."

While this person was a committed member of the congregation, he was totally wrong. He did not understand the righteous demands of God. God is not looking for good intentions; he is seeking a righteousness acceptable to him. This man had no understanding of the teaching of justification by faith. He did not know that Jesus had lived a perfect life on his behalf. By faith he could receive the perfect righteousness of Christ Jesus rather than trusting in his own good intentions. I am sure that many times this man had sung the familiar words of the hymn "Jesus, thy blood and righteousness my beauty are, my glorious dress." Yet he did not understand what those words meant and how they applied to him.

The Gospel Is First

In Christianity, *hearing and believing the Gospel of Jesus Christ is the first step.* All other ingredients associated with being a Christian follow after the Gospel. First, before anything else, God gives us his love, his grace, and his mercy. In order to continually motivate us and prompt us in our Christian life, he continually lavishes upon us his forgiveness and grace.

One day I was talking with a woman about becoming a member of our congregation. She had visited our church from time to time. She said to me, "First I have to learn to love people before I join your church."

"No," I objected. "First you come to church and hear God's Word. As a result you will begin to love people."

"No, I don't think so," she responded. "I am not ready to be a part of a group of caring church people."

I spent an additional ten years in that community. The woman continued to visit our church from time to time, and I continued to speak with her. But she never joined the church because she was never ready. You cannot learn to love; first you must be loved!

A few years ago I got into a conflict with the president of my congregation. We were in the midst of a regular congregational meeting. The subject of financial needs was being discussed. The treasurer commented that there were many who attended church every week but contributed very little money to support the church.

"We have to light a fire under these deadbeats," the president angrily remarked. "We need some good 'money sermons' to get these people to give more." He looked over in my direction.

"We don't get money by preaching money sermons," I responded. "We get money as a result of preaching the Gospel."

"Well, that doesn't work!" he replied.

"If that doesn't work we have no reason to exist as a congregation," I concluded. "If the Gospel doesn't work, we don't need any money."

Before love, before stewardship, before the "Golden Rule," before worship and thanksgiving, we hear the Gospel. Working through the message of the Gospel, the Holy Spirit motivates and causes everything else to take place.

In fact, contrary to the thinking of some Christians, believing the Gospel of Jesus Christ even comes before believing in the truth of the Bible. We believe the Bible as a result of believing the Gospel of Jesus Christ.

PRINCIPLE

Faith receives the benefits of what
God has accomplished in the death and resurrection
of Jesus Christ.

13

◇

The Bible
Is Really True!

◇

*T*he message of the Gospel which we discover in the pages of the Bible, offering the forgiveness of sins, new life on earth, and eternal life in heaven, is the same message that opened eyes, warmed hearts, changed lives, and created the church in the first century. Nothing has changed! God has graciously preserved in truth and purity the good news of his grace in Christ Jesus. Our purpose today is the same as the purpose of the first apostles, prophets, and evangelists: We preach the Gospel.

When a guilty sinner hears the message of the Gospel of Jesus Christ today, the same results take place. Nothing has changed. Eyes are opened, hearts are warmed, and faith is produced in the same way it happened among the first Christians. The miracle of faith is the same for today's sinner as it was for the sinner in the first century. There is no difference in the content or in the results of the message.

Same Message, Different Package

What *has* changed is the way in which the message of the Gospel is packaged. In the first century the apostles, prophets, and evangelists contained the message. They were the vehicles that bore the message. While these first Gospel-preachers used texts from the Old Testament to support the message, the specific content of the Gospel, especially as it related to the Gentiles, came by way of revelation from God.

Because these men bore the revelation, the people would naturally ask, "How do we know that they are trustworthy and that God is indeed speaking his Word through them?" In order to demonstrate that God was with them, he empowered them to perform miracles. They healed the sick and raised the dead.

Today the same message preached by these miracle-working apostles, prophets, and evangelists comes to us in a book. We call the book *THE BIBLE*. The Bible is the container for the message of the Gospel of Jesus Christ. It is the "cradle of Christ."

Today the logical question is not "How do we know that the preachers are trustworthy?" but rather, "How do we know that the Bible, which contains the good news of the Gospel of Jesus Christ, is trustworthy?"

How Do I Know the Bible Is True?

It is not strange, given the modern scientific mindset, that people should ask the question "How do I know the Bible is true?" This is not an unfair question. Many have asked it. If the whole "Christian story" is transmitted to us through the pages of the Bible, the truthfulness of the biblical record is indeed a crucial issue.

If the Bible is not true, must it not follow that the benefits of the death and resurrection of Jesus Christ as revealed to us in the Bible also are not true? Maybe the Moslem religion as revealed in their book, the Koran, is true. Maybe Buddhism is true. There are many who believe and practice it. How do we know the Bible is true?

Contrary to rational thinking, demonstrating the truthfulness of the Gospel of Jesus Christ does not begin by demonstrating the truth of the Bible. This is a very important point. Even though it is logical and reasonable to prove the truth of Christianity by beginning with the reliability of the Bible, *this is not how it works.* The apostle Paul preached the Gospel before it was clearly contained within the pages of the Bible. The epistles of Paul and the other apostles were included within the canon of the New Testament because they spiritually affected the hearts and lives of people.

Of course, if God wished, he could perform miracles through the Bible. If a man was dying of cancer, for example, the Bible could be placed on his body and he would be healed. As a result, everyone would say, "What a wonderful miracle-working book! It must be true."

While God could certainly do this and confirm to us the truth of the Bible, he doesn't do it for a very simple reason: The focus of attention would be on the Bible itself, not on the message of the Gospel that it contains.

So God uses another method to confirm the truth of the Bible: He joins the Bible to the enlightening inner witness of the Holy Spirit. When the Holy Spirit enlightens our minds to understand the Gospel, produces the miracle of faith, and transforms our lives, *he assures us that the entire Bible, which contains that message, is true.*

The problem with many Christians today is that they believe "the salvation message" of the death and resurrection of Jesus Christ *because they find it in the Bible.* They begin by affirming the truth of the Bible. As a result, they might not come to the cross of Christ out of a sense of sin, guilt, failure, and need. Their faith in Jesus is the result of a rational deduction or a conservative mindset bent on preserving the truthfulness of a book, rather than a dynamic, life-changing appropriation of divine grace to help in time of need. For such Christians, the assurance of eternal life is a doctrine to be affirmed rather than a heartfelt, Holy Spirit-confirmed dynamic. In addition, those who accept the "salvation message" because it is found in the Bible might discover that the inner workings of their lives have remained virtually unchanged. While they might be very moral people, their attitudes, motives, and emotions have not been adjusted by the Holy Spirit.

The "faith" of such Christians is always in jeopardy. They are at the mercy of the teachers of evolution and the assaults of modern liberals who seek to discredit the truthfulness of the Bible. The Sunday school faith of many young people has not survived their secular university education because their belief in the death and resurrection of Jesus Christ was merely one domino in a long line. If someone convinces them of the alternative of evolution, raises doubts in their minds over the historical truth of the flood, or claims that the story of Jonah is pure fiction, the message of the Gospel also loses credibility.

I do not deny the value of demonstrating the scientific and logical basis for God as Creator, or providing evidence for the flood, or proving the historicity of the resurrection of Jesus Christ. There are skeptics who will offhandedly reject the Gospel of Jesus Christ simply because they deny the truth of Scripture. Demonstrating the truth of the Bible by providing evidence will remove the stumbling blocks to faith in Jesus Christ, *but it will not create faith in Jesus Christ.*

Nor do I question the necessity for a Christian to affirm the inspiration, inerrancy, and historical truthfulness of the totality of Scripture. There is a unity to Scripture. Would the Holy Spirit dynamically open the eyes of a person to the truth of the Gospel of Jesus Christ and leave him in the dark as to the rest of Scripture? Of course, it is possible that there is a necessary progression that might be taking place. The person who claims to believe the Gospel of Jesus Christ but rejects the Genesis account of creation and the explanation for the fall of man into sin might have a very weak and immature faith, and should be exposed to the hearing of the Gospel and commended to the convincing work of the Holy Spirit. Billy Graham writes:

> There are various reasons for having confidence in the Bible as God's Word, but it is at this point that the work of the Holy Spirit is most plainly manifested. The truth of the matter is that the same Holy Spirit who was the author of the Scriptures . . . also works in each of us to convince us that the Bible is the Word of God to be trusted in all its parts.[1]

Beginning with the Gospel

Some years ago a young man with a Christian background who had been to college for one year and had completed a course in "the Bible as literature" boasted to me of the fact that he was able to disprove some of the stories in the Bible.

He came into my office and arrogantly announced, "I love to argue with you preachers about the Bible. I can prove to you that the Bible contains errors."

He took a seat opposite my desk and with a big smile on his face waited for my response.

After a few moments I responded by asking, "How well do you know the Author?"

"What do you mean?" he somewhat jokingly asked.

"The Holy Spirit is the Author of the Bible. How well do you know him?"

"The Holy Spirit?" he objected. "You're telling me stuff that's found in the Bible. I don't believe that stuff is true."

"The Holy Spirit comes to us and creates faith in our hearts when we hear the message about Jesus and his love for us. I would like to tell you that message. Why don't we kneel down here by my desk?" I got up from behind my desk and moved toward him.

"I will first pray that the Holy Spirit will open your eyes and warm your heart and then I will tell you all about Jesus and what he has done for you. After that we can argue about the Bible."

He quickly got up and left!

If the young man had been burdened by a sense of sin and guilt and would have remained and listened attentively to the message of the Gospel, he might very well have been convinced about the truth of the Bible.

Not Theoretical

While Christian knowledge is gained from the Bible, it is not theoretical knowledge built upon the assumption or theory that what the Bible says is true. While unbelievers may evaluate the Christian's belief in the truth of the Bible as merely being an assumption or a simplistic Sunday school faith, for the Christian whose eyes have been opened by the Holy Spirit this is not the case.

John Calvin speaks about the Holy Spirit's inner witness to the truth of Scripture:

> The same Spirit, therefore, who has spoken through the mouths of the prophets must penetrate into our hearts to persuade us that they faithfully proclaimed what had been divinely

commanded.... Until he illumines their minds, they ever waver among many doubts!... Let this point therefore stand: that those whom the Holy Spirit has inwardly taught truly rest upon Scripture, and that Scripture is indeed self-authenticated; hence, it is not right to subject it to proof and reasonings.

Calvin continues:

Therefore, illumined by his power, we believe neither by our own nor by anyone else's judgment that Scripture is from God.[2]

In one of my evening Bible classes we were discussing the subject of Christian knowledge and certainty. One young woman boldly confessed to the group that she knew for sure that she was going to heaven. Another member of the group objected. The following heated discussion resulted.

"Ah, you can't know that you're going to heaven. Nobody knows for sure that they're going to heaven. It's all speculation anyway."

"You're wrong," the young woman vehemently objected. "We can know that we are saved and forgiven. We can know the Lord! The Bible and the Holy Spirit provide us with that knowledge and certainty. Of course I can't prove it to you, but I do know."

"You think you know," was the reply. "The only things you can know for sure are the things you can see and prove for yourself. Seeing is believing! You're only kidding yourself. You don't know for sure that what the Bible says is true."

"Say whatever you like," she responded with a little smile. "You may not know where *you* are going, but if I died tonight I know for sure that I would be with the Lord."

In listening to the young woman's argument, it was obvious to me that she was not merely defending or clinging to her Sunday school belief in the truthfulness of the Bible. Something very real had occurred in her life to give her such conviction and certainty. The Holy Spirit had opened her eyes through the Gospel and confirmed the truthfulness of the promises of God.

It is the ministry of the Holy Spirit to grant certainty and assurance. Noted nineteenth-century theologian C.F.W. Walther asked the question "Why did God promise and give us his Holy Spirit, if not so that we might become absolutely sure about our own salvation?"[3]

We will not convince doubters of the truth of the Bible and the certainty of eternal life through rational argumentation. I have met people who claim that they became Christians as the result of rejecting the foolish notion of evolution and acknowledging the more logical explanation that God is the Creator. Yet if they use the same rational mentality in approaching the cross of Jesus Christ, the message of the Gospel could possibly remain a mere proposition to be affirmed rather than a life-changing dynamic. We must all come to the cross of Jesus Christ in the same way: as poor, miserable, guilty sinners in need of God's grace and forgiveness!

Word and Spirit

God has given to us the Bible and his Holy Spirit and has intimately joined them together. They cannot be separated! The Word brings the Spirit. The Spirit enlightens our minds through the Word. We know the Bible is true and factual through the Spirit of God, and we know about the Holy Spirit from the Bible. We need the Holy Spirit to understand the Bible so that we might be certain of God's grace and forgiveness. But we need the Bible so that we might know about the Gospel and experience the work of the Holy Spirit.

If you are a scientific investigator evaluating this method of gaining knowledge and certainty, you might say, "This is not reasonable. It is not logical. It is an argument in a circle."

This is true! It is an argument in a circle, but if you are a Christian who has been enlightened by the Holy Spirit, this is truth! Only God our Father could have conceived of such a remarkable method for impacting the lives of his children and granting to them the knowledge and certainty of his love and compassion.

Show Me!

I knew a young man who, as a child, went to a parochial school and faithfully attended Sunday school. When he entered a secular college, his "Sunday school faith" was not sufficient to deal with the assaults of reason, logic, and skepticism. One evening, in the midst of "finals week," tired and confused, he took down his Bible from the shelf and, opening to the beginning of the New Testament, prayed, "Lord, convince me that your Word is true. If you convince me, you can have me." He began to read.

Well, to make a long story short, this young man changed colleges, and attended seminary. Now he and his wife are working in the foreign mission field. The Holy Spirit, enlightening his understanding of the Gospel of Jesus Christ, produced faith. His life was changed. His confusion was replaced by peace. His guilt was removed when the Holy Spirit assured him that his sins were forgiven. As a result, he was convinced that the Bible is truth.

If you doubt the truth of Scripture and have not been convinced by arguments, seek the enlightenment of the Holy Spirit. Pray that the Holy Spirit will open your eyes to the truth.

While there is some value in demonstrating scientific credibility and historical truth, our real task is to preach the Gospel. As a result, the Holy Spirit working through the preaching of the Gospel will lead people to believe the words of the Bible. Our primary job is to give the Holy Spirit the opportunity to convince the gainsayer by preaching the powerful Gospel of Jesus Christ!

PRINCIPLE

*By working through the message
of the Gospel of Jesus Christ, the Holy Spirit
convinces us of the truth of Scripture.*

14

Where Do We

Begin?

---

*R*eal transformation takes place in our lives when we acknowledge our sins, failures, and weaknesses before God and seek his grace to help in time of need. The life-changing grace of God does not come to us *as the result* of our prayer, no matter how fervently we might pray, or *as the result* of some experience with the Holy Spirit, no matter how wonderful that experience might have been. God delivers his grace to us through the means of the Gospel of Jesus Christ. For this reason, the teaching that came out of the Reformation identifies the Gospel as the *means of grace*,[1] or the vehicle through which God works within us in order to create faith and transform our lives.

The dynamic power behind the Gospel of Jesus Christ is the Holy Spirit. Since the words of the Gospel are supernatural divine wisdom, inspired by the Holy Spirit, it is also the purpose of the Holy Spirit to open our eyes to the Gospel as it is revealed in the Bible. As Christians, in whom the Spirit dwells, the Holy Spirit urges us to seek his enlightenment so that we might become ready receivers of his grace and have our hearts open for his work. This combination of the Gospel of Jesus Christ and the Holy Spirit produces life-changing results. According to the apostle Peter, we have been born again through the living and enduring Word of God (1 Peter 1:23). The apostle Paul makes it clear that the Holy Spirit brings Jesus himself to us through the faith-creating Gospel (Romans 10:6-9).

The question is, In seeking the grace of God, where can we clearly discover the meaning and significance of the Gospel of Jesus Christ? Where do we begin? The Bible is a rather large book.

As I shared with you in the opening chapters, I sought the Holy Spirit so that I might understand the power that motivates the Christian life. My experience had been one of defeat. Since this was my need at that time, as I sought the Holy Spirit my eyes were opened to the Gospel promises concerning the work of Jesus Christ found in Galatians 2:20, Romans 6-8, John 15, and Colossians 3:1-3.

I don't know where you are in your understanding of the Christian faith and life, nor do I know what your particular needs might happen to be. Do you understand the truth about your sinful nature? Are you clear on the basis for the forgiveness of your sins? Do you comprehend the truth of justification by faith? Do you have the assurance of eternal life? Do you know that the Christian life is "Not I, but Christ"? Do you know what it means to abide in Christ or walk in the Spirit? As I said before, it is not my purpose to deal with all the spiritual blessings that are offered to us in the Gospel of Jesus Christ. It is my purpose to motivate you to seek God in his Word.

The best place to begin is in the New Testament. We can certainly find the Gospel prefigured in the Old Testament, but it is in the New Testament where it is clearly presented. After being confronted with the Gospel in the New Testament, we can go back to the Old Testament and find there, as Martin Luther put it, Christ on every page. But we must begin with the New Testament.

The New Testament is basically made up of three types of material: narratives, teachings, and admonitions. There are stories about the life and death of Jesus and the development of the early church; teachings about the meaning of the death, and resurrection of the Lord Jesus; and admonitions and instructions for living the Christian life.

If you do not know a great deal about the Person of Jesus Christ and his life upon this earth, it would be good for you to begin with the Gospel of John, which is the simplest and perhaps the most beautiful Gospel.

But most people who attend a Christian church are already familiar with the stories of the life, death, and resurrection of Jesus Christ. Even "twice-a-year" Christians who only attend church on Christmas and Easter are probably aware that Jesus was born in Bethlehem of the Virgin Mary, that he died on the cross, and that he rose from the dead. What they may not know is how those events apply to their lives.

Those who feel that our lives are changed by reading admonitions and directives would suggest that we should primarily study the New Testament to discover the Christian lifestyle. But this is not a good suggestion. While the New Testament admonitions and instructions are very helpful, without the Holy Spirit first enlightening our understanding of the Gospel and teaching us how to live and walk in Christ Jesus, these instructions simply become a new set of laws.

I knew a woman who took very seriously the New Testament instruction "Wives, submit to your husbands" (Ephesians 5:22). One day she said to me, "I'm doing it, but I hate every minute of it." As far as she was concerned, this New Testament instruction was a law that she had to fulfill in order to be a good, obedient Christian.

Her problem was that she was not reading the instruction in the light of the Gospel of Jesus Christ and the operation of the Holy Spirit in her life. Any attitude of submission is not humanly possible until our hearts have been changed through the enlightened knowledge that Jesus submitted to suffering and death on our behalf. What was intended to be an attitude of the Holy Spirit spontaneously at work in her through the Gospel she turned into a law. The result was misery, guilt, and condemnation.

Begin with Romans

If you are already familiar with the life, death, and resurrection of the Lord Jesus, I suggest that you begin with Paul's epistle to the Romans. In that letter we encounter the clearest explanation of what God has done for us through the death and resurrection of Jesus Christ. It is a complete presentation. The truth of Galatians 2:20, for example, can also be clearly discovered in Romans 6.

The content of the book of Romans has had a profound influence upon the history of the Christian church. We know that the Reformation of 1517 began when the Holy Spirit opened Martin Luther's eyes to the concept of the righteousness of God taught by the apostle Paul in Romans 1:17. We know that in 1738 John Wesley experienced life-changing enlightenment after listening carefully to the reading of Martin Luther's introduction to his commentary on the book of Romans. Wesley's heart was "strangely warmed," and what followed was a revival throughout England.

Martin Luther, in his commentary on Romans, explains why this particular book of the Bible has so deeply affected the lives of so many Christians:

> This epistle is really the chief part of the New Testament and the purest Gospel, which not only deserves to be known by heart by a Christian, word for word, but to be studied daily as the daily bread of the soul. It can never be read or studied too much and too well, and the more one deals with it, the more precious it becomes, and the better it tastes.[2]

In reading this quotation from Luther please carefully note that he is not encouraging only theologians and pastors to know the book of Romans. He is writing to Christians in general. He encourages ordinary Christians to commit the words of Romans to memory and to study the epistle every day.

To be even more specific, I suggest that you concentrate your immediate attention upon the first eight chapters of Romans. While this is not a great deal of reading, these chapters contain the most complete presentation of the Gospel of Jesus Christ that you will find in the Bible. The apostle also presents the truth in consecutive fashion, building one truth upon the previous truth. He begins with the universality of sin, then moves into forgiveness and justification, speaking of our nature as being "in Adam" and dealing with our death to sin through baptism and our new life in Christ. In chapters 6–8 he profoundly expresses the conflicts that continue between our new nature in Christ and the "old Adam," and teaches us how to live in the Spirit so that there is "no longer any condemnation for those who are in Christ Jesus." There are many blessings to be uncovered in those eight chapters.

Don't Forget About Enlightenment!

Don't forget one thing: You will not understand the first eight chapters of the book of Romans without the enlightenment of the Holy Spirit. Martin Luther didn't. The Holy Spirit had to open his eyes to what the "righteousness of God" was all about. John Wesley didn't. It was the Holy Spirit who warmed his heart. The Holy Spirit will also have to enlighten your understanding. So don't forget to pray!

I have a large bookmark in my Bible that extends beyond the covers of the book. On the top of the bookmark, which is always visible, I have written the words "PRAY FOR THE HOLY SPIRIT!" I can never have enough visible reminders to pray for the Holy Spirit to enlighten the words of the Bible. I would suggest that you do the same thing. Make your own personal cardboard bookmark. Write on it something like "Pray for the Holy Spirit" or "Come, Holy Spirit, and open my eyes and change my life."

In reading the first eight chapters of Romans, I would encourage you to purchase a good Bible dictionary. There are some strange words that you might encounter, particularly justification, redemption, atonement, and reconciliation. Some translations of the Bible might also include expiation or propitiation. Understanding the meaning of these terms is very important.

I found the book *The Normal Christian Life*, by Chinese evangelist Watchman Nee, to be very helpful. He especially deals with the first eight chapters of Romans. I would encourage you to purchase a copy. But keep in mind that you will not understand the teachings of Romans 1-8 just because Nee did. Nor will you understand justification by faith because Luther and Calvin did. The Holy Spirit must personally enlighten your understanding and make these truths relevant to you so that your heart is affected.

The Instrument for Church Renewal

There is deep concern today about the conditions in many Christian congregations. Church membership, attendance, and stewardship are declining. Many great congregations that were raised up in the 40's and 50's are but a shell of their former existence. A heart cry for renewal is going up to God in behalf of apathetic and declining congregations.

Numerous "renewing" efforts have been undertaken, with varying degrees of success. Although some popular movements have produced growing congregations, the emphasis has often been placed upon spiritual experience, entertaining worship services, support groups, fellowship activities, and the like.

Why don't we to turn to our Bible and use it as an instrument for church renewal? Do we not believe that the Holy Spirit releases his power through the Gospel of Jesus Christ? If the Holy Spirit, through the Book of Romans, initiated the great Reformation of 1517 and the eighteenth-century revival in England, will he not do the same thing for us today?

Christian congregations would experience a great revival and renewal if the members dedicated themselves to knowing the first eight chapters of Romans.

Of course, after you read and study the first eight chapters of Romans and experience the dynamic enlightenment of the Holy Spirit, you will want to study the rest of the Bible as well.

PRINCIPLE

*We study the Bible
in order to discover what God has done
for us in Christ Jesus. The Gospel
is the center of Scripture.*

15

◇

*Chewing
on the Word*

◇

*S*ince the the Person of the Holy Spirit is at work enlightening our understanding of the Bible, it is a unique book. For this reason, the way in which we read the Bible is also unique. We cannot beneficially read the Bible, especially the first eight chapters of Romans, in the same way we would seek to understand words and gain information by reading a novel or a newspaper. We are not alone when we are reading the Bible. Another Person, the Person of the Holy Spirit, is involved with us. While he is waiting for us to read, we wait for him to enlighten. The Bible is a book for careful meditation.

Bible Stories

Of course, there are many sections in the Bible, such as stories of Old Testament heroes and heroines or incidents in the life of Jesus, that might be read like a short story. Such stories offer interesting and important reading. Many of you are probably already familiar with a good number of Bible stories. Through these narratives we gain insight into our relationship with God. Even though Bible stories may be easy reading, the Holy Spirit still works through them, seeking to draw an application to our own lives.

Bible stories are especially effective in teaching children. Perhaps you recall learning Bible stories from your Sunday school days and taking home your leaflet with the full-color picture on the cover depicting the heroic acts of Moses, Joshua, or David. In my mind I can still see the picture of Daniel praying in the lion's den.

But while Bible stories are valuable because they teach us about our relationship with God, the real solid food or meat is found in the teaching sections of the Bible, especially in the New Testament epistles such as Romans. Here we encounter the all-important application of the death and resurrection of the Lord Jesus Christ to our lives. We discover the mystery of the Gospel.

If we think of Bible stories as the milk of the Word because they are easy to read and digest, the New Testament epistles, such as Paul's letter to the Romans, are the meat of the Word. They are meat because we have to chew on them. They cannot be immediately swallowed and digested.

Meditating on the Word

If you begin to read the first eight chapters of the book of Romans, you will encounter many "meaty" verses that demand a great deal of "chewing." When I speak of "chewing on the Word," I mean to *reflect upon, think about, or ponder* the content of one or two verses, or to *meditate upon* the Word of God.

In order for the Holy Spirit to effectively open our eyes and enlighten our minds, we must focus our conscious, undivided attention upon the Word and take the time to think about what we are reading. This is what it means to meditate. We give the Holy Spirit time to work with us. Often I will take a single verse of Scripture and think about it. I may do this while driving in the car, or walking the dog, or simply sitting in a chair drinking a cup of coffee.

Today the word "meditation," like the word "enlightenment," has different applications. Transcendental Meditation or TM involves the emptying of the mind of all thoughts and repeating a mantra, which is a Hindu prayer or invocation in the Sanskrit language. The person repeating the mantra over and over again has no idea what he is saying. Buddhism and mysticism also promote an empty-minded form of meditation.

In contrast, when Christians meditate upon the Word of God this does not involve maintaining a blank mind. Rather, it means filling the mind. When we hear the Word of God preached or taught, or when we are engaged in our own private Bible reading, we meditate upon the Word to allow the Holy Spirit the opportunity to open our eyes and enlighten our understanding.

Let me share with you a simple technique that I have found very helpful in meditating upon the Word of God.

"For Me!"

Many people make the mistake of regarding the words of the Bible as being written to a specific people living many years ago. This is one of the reasons they have difficulty practically applying the words of the Bible to themselves today. Even when we pastors teach the Bible we often get too hung up on the conditions and special circumstances of the day in which the words were written, rather than concentrating upon the application of the Word to the hearts of people today. While it is certainly true that understanding the conditions of the day gives us insight into the application of the Word to the people of that day, what we need to clearly understand is how the Word applies to us today.

In order to make that application, I have found it very helpful to read Bible verses as if they were written specifically to me. Let me show you what I mean.

Let's use the theme verses of the book of Romans, chapter 1, verses 16 and 17. As you begin reading and meditating upon the first eight chapters of Romans, these two verses will provide you with the first big "chunk of meat." As we consider the verses, I will ask you questions about the verses. You think about the questions, and provide the answers. Read carefully the verses:

> I am not ashamed of the gospel, because it is the power of God for the salvation of everyone who believes: first for the Jew, then for the Gentile. For in the gospel a righteousness from God is revealed, a righteousness that is by faith from first to last, just as it is written: "The righteous will live by faith."

We first pray, "Lord, by your Holy Spirit enlighten my understanding of your Word. Open my eyes that I might see. Make your Word a personal, life-changing word written specifically to me."

The verse begins, "I am not ashamed of the gospel." Of course, the "I" is the apostle Paul, but *is it not also you?* Put your name in place of the "I" and boldly confess: "(Your name) is not ashamed of the Gospel."

Further, take out the word "everyone" and replace it with your name. The verse would then read: "(Your name) is not ashamed of the gospel because it is the power of God for the salvation of (your name) who believes."

The Gospel is God's power! Think about that. If you want God's power at work in your life, where do you go? Where do you look? The Gospel is the power to save you. Save you from what?

You are included in the "everyone." Are you a believer? Then you are saved.

The apostle says that the Gospel reveals *a righteousness from God* that is totally by faith. To whom does the Gospel reveal this "righteousness from God" which is by faith? Obviously, it is revealed to *you*. Confess that fact: "The Gospel tells me that I am righteous!"

The verse ends, "The righteous will live by faith." God has declared you righteous. Put your name in there. You live by faith! Faith in what? What is the alternative to living by faith?

By personalizing those two simple verses you not only hear a word spoken to you, but you also hear yourself confessing your faith and claiming the promises as your very own.

You will discover many great "chunky" promises that God has made to you in the first eight chapters of the book of Romans. Chew upon those promises. Personalize them. Meditate upon them. Read the verses as if the apostle were writing his letter directly to you. Allow the Holy Spirit to speak to you through the Word.

Take, for example, the simple verse from Romans 6:23: "The wages of sin is death, but the gift of God is eternal life in Christ Jesus our Lord." Consider the following personal thoughts gleaned from that verse.

The first part of the verse tells me that my sin pays a wage. What does that mean? This is a specific cause-and-effect reality. My sin pays the wage of death. My death will demonstrate that I am a sinner. That's interesting. The thought that comes to mind is this: The one true fact you can declare about me at my funeral is: "He was a sinner!"

But God has given to me the free gift of eternal life in Jesus Christ. This is a gift! How do I respond to a free gift? Can I earn it? Pay for it? Or do I simply receive it? Obviously, I can only receive it since it is free. Have I received the free gift? Yes! Definitely! The Holy Spirit has given me faith. How do I respond? Thank you, Lord!

So while it is true that my sin pays the wage of death, my God gives to me a free gift of eternal life through Jesus Christ.

When you meditate upon the Word of God, make it your own personal word, because it is intended to be personal. *It's for you!* It applies to you. It speaks about your situation.

As you read and meditate upon God's Word and the Holy Spirit opens your eyes, you will discover many changes taking place in your life. Your attitudes toward life will change. Your bitterness or resentment will dissipate. Your worries and fears will be replaced with faith. Joy will be stirred within your life. You will be "truly transformed" by the living and active Word of God.

Hearing the Word

Praying for the enlightenment of the Holy Spirit and meditating can also be done when you are listening to the reading of the Word of God or to the sermon. When you sit in church, if you want to get anything out of what is happening, you have to put something into it. You cannot listen to the sermon, sing the words of the hymns, and hear the reading of the Scripture lessons as you would, for example, listen to your car radio.

Effective listening in church demands meditating upon and pondering the words that are being spoken. If the words go in one ear and out the other, we are the ones who are losing the benefit of those words.

To hear the Word of God means that you are consciously focused so that you meditate upon and ponder the words that are being spoken and sung. In other words, don't just sit there as a "pewpotato" who is merely fulfilling a religious duty by going to church. Be actively engaged in hearing the Word of God.

The most important time in the Sunday morning service is when the clear message of the Gospel of Jesus Christ is being proclaimed. It is the time for you to put away all other thoughts and concerns and attentively listen, breathe a prayer for enlightenment, and allow the Holy Spirit to graciously work in your mind and in your heart. (If you happen to attend a church in which the clear Gospel of Jesus Christ is not proclaimed on a Sunday morning, I would encourage you to speak to your pastor. If nothing changes, find a new church where the Gospel is preached. It is your right to hear the Gospel on a Sunday morning. It is your responsibility before God to be in a place where that Gospel is clearly proclaimed.)

If you have difficulty concentrating upon the Word of God and there are empty pews in the front of the church, which there usually are, move up so that nothing will come between you and what is being proclaimed. I realize that many of you have been sitting in the same pew for years. Perhaps a change would be a good way to develop the practice of prayerfully and attentively listening.

Fight for your right to hear the Gospel of Jesus Christ! If you are not able to hear because the sound system doesn't work, or if there are too many distractions, you have the right and obligation to do something about it.

A Good Reason for Complaint

An elderly gentleman from my congregation was very hard-of-hearing. When our church was built, some 60 years ago, "hearing aids" were installed in four of the pews. Well, the hearing aids eventually failed, and since the wires had been imbedded in the concrete floor, the system was nonrepairable.

This gentleman complained! Every Sunday the ushers were verbally blasted. The church secretary received two or three somewhat nasty phone calls each week. In response to his complaints, the Board of Directors purchased, at a rather sizable expense, a wireless setup for the hearing impaired, but the man never got to use it. Before the system was installed, the Lord called him home.

At his funeral I preached on the words from Romans 10:17: "Faith comes from hearing." I asked the question, "Did our brother in Christ desire to hear the Gospel of Jesus Christ?" Of course, the answer was a resounding YES! I told the story of the broken hearing aids and his response. His desire to hear the Word of God was clear evidence that the Holy Spirit was at work in his life. On the basis of that desire, I could declare that he believed in the Lord Jesus and was in heaven because the Gospel works!

It is especially exciting for the one preaching the Gospel to see people intently involved in hearing. I have one man in my congregation who hangs on every word that I speak. It is encouraging for me to watch his expressions of excitement and joy over the Good News of the Gospel. Every Sunday morning at the door, he has a very insightful comment to make about the content of the sermon.

By personal interaction with this man, I have come to know his deep faith. Why does he have such faith? Because he attentively hears the Word of God. If everyone in my congregation listened the way that man listened, our congregational life and ministry would be profoundly renewed. Why? Because there is spiritual life and power in God's Word.

Listen Carefully

Throughout the course of Sunday morning service, there are numerous opportunities to receive from God.

When the Scripture lessons for the day are about to be read, breathe a short prayer: "Holy Spirit, open my eyes and speak to me through these words." Listen to what is being read. If the words of the lessons are printed in the Sunday bulletin, read them very carefully along with the oral reading.

When you receive the Lord's Supper, concentrate on the words "Given and shed for me for the remission of my sins." The benefits of communion are not received through the eating and drinking, but are received by faith in the Word and promises of God.

When hymns are being sung, concentrate specifically upon the words. Some of the most beautiful explanations of the Gospel of Jesus Christ are found in our hymns. Don't look around at the other people or be self-conscious of your singing voice. Concentrate upon the words. For example, think deeply about the following hymn verse:

> My hope is built on nothing less than Jesus' blood and righteousness. No merit of my own I claim, but wholly lean on Jesus' name. On Christ the solid rock I stand; all other ground is sinking sand.

This is a magnificent explanation of the Gospel of Jesus Christ. Much of our hymns are rich in meaning. Think deeply about the words as you sing them.

I always remind my choir director about the importance of the words that are being sung by the choir. If the people in the congregation are not able to understand the words of the choral selection, the choir might just as well be singing "Mary had a little lamb" or "Row, row,

row your boat." While the music may stir the emotions, it is the Word that stirs faith.

The most dangerous moments in a Sunday morning worship service are when you are reciting words that you know by heart. It is here that you can easily become guilty of the sin of vain and empty babbling. Remind yourself to focus upon what is being said.

Faith Comes by Hearing

In Romans 10:17 the apostle Paul tells us that faith is produced as a result of hearing the "word" or "message" of Christ. The word in Greek used for "message" is *rhematos*, which means a direction or personal instruction. In other words, our faith does not increase as the result of having words thrown at us. It is not automatic. Faith is strengthened and increased by hearing a very *personal* message. Therefore, carefully listen!

It is the will of God that all people who are confronted with the messsage of the Gospel of Jesus Christ on a Sunday morning hear the message, have their eyes opened to the Good News about Jesus, cling in faith to him, and go home rejoicing.

Why doesn't this happen? According to one seventeenth-century German theologian:

> The most gracious God seriously designs to illuminate all men, but only they are actually illuminated who, called and led to the church, receive the grace of the Holy Spirit, and listen attentively to the divine Word, read it, and meditate upon it. . . . For the sinner if obstinately perverse, may hinder the supernatural illumination of the Holy Spirit.[1]

Many people do not understand and cling to the message of the Gospel of Jesus Christ because they do not prayerfully and attentively listen to what is being preached. There are many distractions. The devil is continually at work to fill the mind of the hearer with other thoughts and concerns. If he cannot stop you from going to church on a Sunday morning, he will try to stop you from listening. The Word of God can be resisted by simply turning it off.

I have heard people say, "I didn't get anything out of that church service." The reason is that they didn't listen! They didn't put anything into it.

PRINCIPLE

Since God changes our lives by his living and active Word, we should pay very close attention to it and meditate upon it.

16

---◇---

Facts,

Not Feelings

---◇---

*A*s you seek the enlightenment of the Holy Spirit and meditate upon the words of the Gospel, your life and experience are going to be affected. Your faith will grow. As a result, joy and peace will fill your heart. Any person who attentively hears the Gospel or prayerfully meditates upon God's promises will receive such results. It is the inevitable effect of God's Word. The Holy Spirit guarantees such results. *The Word of God will produce positive, life-changing spiritual experiences.*

Different terms are often used by Christians to define their life-changing experiences with the Lord Jesus. This results in much confusion. Some speak of a "salvation" experience. Others talk about being "born again" or "filled with the Holy Spirit." Some say that their lives were changed when they "prayed to accept Christ," or "made a decision for Jesus," or "let Jesus into their heart," or "asked Jesus to rule on the throne of their heart." Some talk about letting Jesus be "Lord of their life." I have heard people claim to have experienced "the joy of the Lord," or being filled with "the peace that passes all understanding," or having a "cleansed conscience."

The fact is that *we come to faith in Jesus Christ and experience his life-changing grace as the result of the Holy Spirit opening our eyes to the truth of the Gospel of Jesus Christ.* There is no other way that God transforms lives and makes Christians! No matter what you call it, the dynamic is still the same: Your life was changed because Christ died and rose again for you. The Holy Spirit changed your life when you heard the Word of truth, the Gospel of your salvation, and he brought you to faith (Ephesians 1:13). Be sure to properly place your focus. It is very important.

For this reason, I believe that the enlightenment of the Holy Spirit is the spiritual experience and dynamic behind all awakenings, revivals, renewals and reformations in the church. The Holy Spirit gives light. He opens our eyes to the Word of God and creates faith. As a result our lives are transformed and spiritual revival breaks out among God's people. *There is no revival in the church without changed lives. There are no changed lives without the Holy Spirit. And there is no working of the Holy Spirit apart from the Word of God.*

Facts, Faith and Experience

Understanding the relationship between the Word of God and personal life-changing experience is very important. For example, in a previous chapter we meditated upon Romans 6:23: "The wages of sin is death, but

the gift of God is eternal life in Christ Jesus our Lord."
When your eyes are opened to the truth that heaven is a
gift, you are filled with peace and joy. You know that you
have eternal life. If someone would ask you the question
"How do you know you are going to heaven?" you
would not say, "I know I am going to heaven because I
am filled with peace and joy." Rather, you would properly say, "I know I am going to heaven *because the Bible
says that heaven is a free gift*." In case you should ever lose
your assurance, peace, and joy, you would simply go
back to the same Word and promise of God regarding
eternal life, and the Holy Spirit would do his work of
assurance again.

I once asked a person the question "How can you be
sure your sins are forgiven?"

He responded, "Because my conscience is clear?"

This is a wrong understanding. A clear conscience is
the *result* of knowing that Jesus died for you. While the
condition of your conscience may change, the benefits
that come through the cross of Jesus Christ remain the
same. Therefore, if our conscience bothers us, we go
back to the good news of the Gospel. The Word and
promises of God never change.

I heard it put this way: Fact, faith, and experience were
walking on top of a wall. As long as faith kept looking at
the facts found in the Word of God, experience always
came running along behind. But as soon as faith looked
back to see whether experience was coming, both faith
and experience fell off the wall. Therefore, keep your
eyes on the facts. Focus upon the Word of God, not on
your experience.

Looking in the Wrong Place

As a result of using questionable definitions for life-
changing Christian experience, the possiblity of doubt
arising is very real. For example, a few years ago I wrote a

book titled *Christ-Esteem,* in which I discussed the sufficiency of the Person and work of Jesus Christ for life and salvation. I clearly explained that the assurance of the forgiveness of sins and eternal salvation was based upon the historical fact of the death and resurrection of Jesus Christ recorded in the Bible, and not upon personal experience. We know that we are saved, forgiven, and heaven-bound not because of our faith or experience but because the Bible tells us that Jesus died and rose again.

One day I received a phone call from a pastor of a large congregation in the South. He had read the book and had some questions. He was a member of a particular denomination that taught people to answer an altar call, come forward, and "get saved."

After identifying himself and his reason for calling, he very bluntly asked, "When were you saved?"

"When Jesus died on the cross and rose again," I answered confidently.

"What about your experience? Have you had any experience?"

"Of course I've had experience!" I responded. "My sins are forgiven. My conscience is clear. I am a new creature in Christ and know that I am going to heaven."

For a few moments there was silence. Somehow he was stumped by my response. And then, somewhat more gently, he began to share his problem.

"Twenty-five years ago I had a glorious salvation experience," he began. "I got saved. I was born again. My life was totally changed. I decided to become a pastor and worked very hard at building a large congregation."

He paused and then continued with some hesitation, "Now ... as a result of some personal problems ... I am no longer sure that I have ever really been saved or born again."

His voice reflected a deep sense of discouragement and disappointment. He continued, "What you said in your book about the certainty of salvation being based upon facts and not upon experience was very interesting."

I felt sorry for the man. I knew it was very difficult for him to make such a confession to another pastor who was not even a part of his denomination.

I responded to him gently, yet with confidence.

"My friend, your problem is that you are looking for the certainty of your salvation in the wrong place," I explained to him. "You are looking at your experience. You didn't get saved when you went forward in response to an altar call. You were saved as a result of the death and resurrection of Jesus Christ, not as a result of your feelings. Keep focused upon what God has done for you in Jesus Christ, not upon how you responded. Keep your eyes on the promises of God, not on your personal experience, be it positive or negative. Confess to yourself the truth of the Gospel of Jesus Christ. Jesus died for you. He shed his blood for you. No experience in your life can change that reality."

We spoke at length about the nature of Christian knowledge and certainty. Even though his life-changing experience of 25 years earlier was a legitimate Christian experience, it could not be used as a basis for the certainty of forgiveness and salvation.

It is the purpose of God to call us back to his Word so that the Holy Spirit can strengthen and bolster our faith, which always needs bolstering. If we ever doubt any of the promises of God and experience fear, guilt, or worry, we should turn back to the Bible and again read and meditate upon the promises of God. As a result, the Holy Spirit will again enlighten our eyes and rekindle the certainty of God's love, grace, and forgiveness.

For this reason we preach the same message of Christ crucified, risen, ascended, and coming again Sunday after Sunday after Sunday. We always need to be reminded to turn our eyes upon Jesus—the Jesus of the New Testament who died for us and rose again.

Continual Process

As you begin to become more and more familiar with promises of the Gospel and even have your favorite texts committed to memory, you will discover that the enlightenment of the Holy Spirit is a continual experience. You will never arrive at the place of depleting the light of the Spirit upon God's Word. No one has ever "mastered" the Bible or truthfully boasted, "I know it all." As one theologian put it:

> Ordinary illumination is not accomplished instantaneously, but by intervals, by degrees, by acts frequently repeated, that man may be disposed and prepared to admit continuously more and more light of truth.[1]

The Holy Spirit will even shed more and more light upon sections of Scripture that may be very familiar to you. For example, I am amazed each year when it comes time to prepare sermons for Christmas, Lent, Easter, or Ascension. Invariably I discover new things about the Lord Jesus that I had never seen before. This affects my life. Even though I had used these sections from the Bible many times before, yet the Holy Spirit always sheds more light which always affects my life.

In his book *The Holy Spirit*, Billy Graham shares his own experience of the continual enlightenment of the Holy Spirit:

> Things I may have known intellectually for years have come alive to me in their fuller significance almost miraculously. As I have studied the Scriptures, I have also learned that the Spirit always lets more light shine from the Word. Almost every time I read an old familiar passage I see something new. This happens because the written Word of God is a living

Word. I always come to the Scriptures with the Psalmist's prayer, "Open my eyes that I may see wonderful things from Thy law."[2]

There are also times when we may have studied a section of Scripture, but our knowledge is a mere "top-of-the-head" knowledge. Through the ongoing enlightenment of the Holy Spirit, that knowledge will move from the head into the heart. William Hordern clearly explains the nature of this experience:

> A person may have been taught a system of theological ideas and may believe them, but such belief may be merely a top-of-the-head acceptance. But the day may come when such a person has an experience in depth through which the beliefs already held become more vivid, real and decisive for the person. In short, there is a great difference between knowing something because we have been told about it and knowing the same thing because we have experienced it for ourselves.[3]

Many theologically trained pastors have shared with me this same kind of experience. I heard a pastor jokingly explain his ever-increasing baldness by saying that the Holy Spirit had to continually hit him on the top of the head to move his doctrines from his head to his heart.

PRINCIPLE

*Our lives are transformed
by the facts that we discover in the
Gospel of Jesus Christ.
Keep your focus upon those facts.*

17

*Pastors, Theologians,
and Church Custodians*

*O*ne afternoon I was heading out the church door when I heard someone calling to me from the front of the church, "Pastor! Are you in a hurry? I would like to talk to you for a few minutes."

It was the custodian, Marie, who was busily dusting the church pews.

"Sure, Marie," I responded. "What can I do for you?"

I walked up to the front of the church and sat down on one of the pews.

Marie was a very pleasant person, probably in her late sixties. She and her husband, Ernie, lived across the street from the church and served as our custodians. Marie was not an educated person. She had probably never gone to high school. Over the past months, as a result of my new understanding of the Christian life, I had been preaching and teaching in Bible class that Christ dwells within the life of the Christian and that through him we can experience a new life in the Spirit.

"I want to tell you about something that is very exciting," she began. "I have never understood what Paul was talking about in Romans 8. You know the verses. He says that the spirit of life in Christ has set us free from sin and death, and that we obey the law by walking in the Spirit."

I nodded in agreement.

"I have been thinking about those verses and praying that the Holy Spirit would teach me, and you know what? I finally understand what Paul means."

I began to smile, excited to see the eyes of a Christian opening up to the truth in God's Word.

"If the life of Christ is living in me," Marie explained, "I have everything. It is his life in me that changes me. It is not my effort. His life in me sets me free from sin and death. Isn't that right?"

"That's right," I agreed. "Isn't that a great truth?"

"I just had to tell you that. I never realized that studying the Bible could be so exciting."

Marie concluded, turned away, and picked up her dustcloth from the pew. She seemed almost embarrassed to have taken up my time by telling me about something she learned from the Bible. She didn't realize that for a pastor, hearing such a testimony from one of your members provides the greatest satisfaction and joy.

"Marie, you made my day!" I assured her, and went back about my business.

A few months later I was visiting at a theological seminary as a part of a group of Charismatic pastors meeting with some of the professors to discuss the work of the Holy Spirit. In the course of the conversation one of the professors, a noted doctor of theology, said, "I do have to admit to you brethren that I don't understand Romans 8."

I couldn't help but smile a little, but I wisely kept my mouth shut. I'm sure that the brotherly discussion would not have been encouraged if I would have declared, "You don't understand Romans 8? My church custodian understands Romans 8!"

The point is that a church custodian, enlightened by the Holy Spirit, can see more than a theologian who may possibly be depending upon his intellectual skill in order to gain understanding. "What is hidden from the wise is often revealed to babes."

Who Needs Theologians?

If we are able to know and understand the Bible through the enlightenment of the Holy Spirit, and if we are able to experience a new life in Jesus Christ by simply meditating upon the Gospel of Jesus Christ, why in the world do we need pastors and theologians? For that matter, is there any value whatsoever to a "theological" education?

These questions are widely debated, especially among those who have had a spiritual experience or awakening. I have known Pentecostals and Charismatics who disdain the professional clergy, regarding them merely as "Chief Executive Officers" of institutions rather than spiritual leaders. The early Pentecostals were known to declare, "We don't need no book learnin'. We got da Holy Ghost."

What is the relationship between you, the Holy Spirit, the Bible, and your pastor? If you are able to understand the Gospel of Jesus Christ through the enlightenment of the Holy Spirit, why do you need a pastor? What is the value of a theological education? If a person's mind is enlightened by the Holy Spirit, what's wrong with the clergy that they need to go to seminary?

Both the Holy Spirit and Sound Theology

If we think that understanding the truth in the Bible requires a theological education, we are badly mistaken. If this were true, only the theologically educated could receive any life-changing benefit from reading the Bible. The rest of us would be doomed to reading self-help books. Of course, that would also leave out my little Lithuanian grandmother who hungered for and frequently read and studied her Bible. What is worse, we would be guilty of belittling the work of the Holy Spirit, who enlightens the mind of any person engaged in prayerfully reading and studying the Word.

But on the other hand, we are also wrong if we consider a theological education to be of no value. Seminaries train the pastor to study the Scriptures in their original languages, interpret the verses of Scripture on the basis of sound principles, and formulate clear teaching on the basis of the Word of God.

For two or three years following my experience with the Holy Spirit, which I later defined as enlightenment, I saw the eyes of people, like Marie, opening up to the truth of the Gospel of Jesus Christ. As a result, I began to disdain theological education and theologians. I became a "theologian basher," criticizing anything associated with the institutional church. What's more, I felt entirely justified in doing so, believing that I had been robbed by a religious system that magnified natural intellect while ignoring spiritual reality. Every theological journal that arrived in my mailbox found the wastebasket. As far as I was concerned it took a wise man to make complicated truths simple, but only idiots make simple truths complicated.

Then one evening I heard a testimony which totally changed my viewpoint about the value of a theological education.

Every Sunday evening we had a prayer and praise gathering. Anywhere from 50 to 100 people came together to sing, pray, and share.

One week Richie, a young man from a neighboring community, shared his testimony. He asked us to pray for him, explaining, "I finally enrolled in night school so I can learn to read. I am embarrassed to tell you this, but I can't read the Bible. Oh, I carry my Bible with me"—and he held up his Bible—"but I can't read it. I so badly want to be able to learn so I can read it. Please pray for me that the Lord will help me to learn."

After Richie had finished, the thought struck me, "Learning how to read is a pure intellectual exercise!"

I could not argue with that conclusion. There is nothing "spiritual" about vocabulary and grammar. Obviously, I encouraged him to go to school to learn to read the Bible, but as a result my mind was changed about the value of theological education.

If it is necessary to learn how to read, how to understand vocabulary and grammar, in order to gain understanding of the words of the Bible, why shouldn't a person learn Greek and Hebrew to read the Bible in its original language? Why shouldn't a person learn how to interpret the words, understand the context, deal with the nuances of the literature, review the history of doctrinal formulations on the basis of the literature, learn every type of skill related to the use of Scripture, and become "a workman that needs not to be ashamed"?

Because of Richie's testimony, a few months later I offered a course in the fundamentals of the Greek language. Twenty-five serious Bible students from my congregation in a small town in Michigan wanted to study Greek. I also offered a course in hermeneutics. We studied the historical principles for biblical interpretation.

I don't know if Richie ever learned how to read. I certainly hope that he did. He only came to our church on two or three occasions. I do know that his simple testimony influenced the direction of my life and ministry. As a result of his intellectual pursuit, I threw myself into a study of doctrine and theology.

I have come to truly appreciate those who have spent years in the study of doctrine and theology. In fact, I earnestly "covet" their knowledge. An enlightened theologian will obviously be able to see more clearly and understand more deeply the truth taught in the Bible than will an enlightened church custodian. Martin Luther, himself a trained doctor of theology, is referred to as a "highly enlightened man."[1] May our Lord provide our churches with many "enlightened theologians" whose lives reflect the transforming power of the Gospel of Jesus Christ.

But a seminary education also has inherent dangers. Since the Bible is a document written in human language, it is possible to approach that document equipped with only a trained theological intellect. While the Holy Spirit is linked to the Bible, theologians may read and study it without their hearts being open to his enlightening work. Martin Luther said that those who come to the Bible and trust only in their own intellect to understand are like "pigs who rush in with dirty feet." As a result of trusting in the intellect, the Bible becomes a dead, lifeless, and at times boring document.

Correctly Handling the Word of Truth

People do not enroll in seminaries or Bible colleges to learn the content of the Bible. Before anyone enrolls in a seminary he should already know the content of the Bible. The seminary does not teach the future pastor "the Word of truth." Rather, as the apostle Paul wrote to Timothy, the seminary teaches the future pastor how to "correctly handle the Word of truth."

The pastor in your congregation is not supposed to know the content of the Bible for you. As a Christian, you should know that for yourself. This is the responsibility of every Christian. The pastor is there to teach you, guide you, and direct you so that, as you learn more and more of the Bible, you do not go astray in the manner in which you "handle the Word of truth."

As you begin to study the Bible for yourself and pray for the enlightenment of the Holy Spirit, you will especially need your pastor. I have witnessed much confusion among people who have been spiritually enlightened and as a result think they know it all. Many Christians have been led astray into strange and perverted teachings by disdaining the role and function of a Christian pastor. Others have been damaged spiritually because they committed themselves to "pastors" who have not been trained to discern truth from error. Knowing the Bible does not make a person a pastor, any more than knowing how to operate an automobile makes a person an auto mechanic.

The purpose of the Christian ministry is never more clearly seen than when the members of the congregation are studying and discussing the Gospel of Jesus Christ. It is then that the role of the pastor becomes very important. There are many faithful pastors who wish that issues in their congregation were centered on the Scriptures rather than on meaningless debates over meaningless subjects. Would it not be exciting to spend time in congregational business meetings discussing the meaning of various chapters and verses from the Bible rather than debating over what color to paint the parish hall or arguing over the budget?

PRINCIPLE

*Even though the Holy Spirit
enlightens our understanding of the Word of God,
we should still "study to show ourselves
approved, as workmen who need not
to be ashamed."*

18

◇

Words
to Live By

*T*he Word of God has a very practical benefit. It does more than merely impart historical information or provide doctrinal knowledge. It is a "Word to live by." We are not merely *informed* by the words of the Bible, but we are *formed* or *transformed* by the Gospel of Jesus Christ which is revealed to us in the Bible. The Word of God renews our minds and changes our lives.

When we meditate upon the promises of God, memorize key Bible passages, and daily remind ourselves of what God has done for us in Christ Jesus, the Holy Spirit is granting us light, enabling us to walk securely in the midst of this world. The psalmist declares, "Thy Word is a lamp unto my feet and a light unto my path." Without that light, life is without purpose or meaning, or, as one philosopher put it, "a tale told by an idiot."

The Information Age

Never before has a knowledge of God's Word been as necessary as it is today. We are caught up in the midst of an explosion of information. Our attitudes, our reactions, our views of life are readily formed by the abundance of words and information that we daily receive. Without a knowledge of God's Word, we have difficulty sorting things out. What is truth? What is deception? What is our nature? Why are we here? Where are we going?

Years ago, before the advent of the mass media, life was much simpler. For many people living in rural communities and small towns, the only institutions that imparted knowledge and information were the church and the school. The pastor's Sunday morning sermon became a weekly media event.

Today, when it comes to presenting a philosophy of life, promoting a lifestyle, establishing a purpose for daily living, and discussing morals, ethics, and values, the real influence is provided by the likes of Phil Donahue, Oprah Winfrey, "Sixty Minutes," or even "Love Connection."

Tossed To and Fro . . .

Devoid of an understanding of life, many people have no idea what they believe. They pursue fads, read the newest self-help books, or dabble in weird, New Age practices. They believe the latest thing the world throws at them. For this reason they are defeated by the situations of life. Their fleeting joy and peace is purely circumstantial. It is the evening network news that establishes a hope for the future. Morals and ethics are determined by soap operas. Madison Avenue provides a value system. Personal security is based not upon God, who has made many great promises, but upon the economic forecast and political climate.

Many ideas promoted and widely accepted today, even by Christians, do not in any way agree with the truth of God's Word. We hear about the "Fatherhood of God and the brotherhood of man." People say, "Whatever will be, will be." We often regard ourselves as being "victims of circumstances." When it comes to our work and accomplishments, we think that "God helps those who help themselves." We are supposed to "do our own thing" and make "our own choice." If we do not want to accept blame, we can say, "The devil made me do it" or "I was abused as a child, so I'm not responsible." Many have adopted the philosophy of life found in the statement "If it feels good, do it!" Secular humanists tells us that "man is the measure of all things." Evolutionists say that "accidents happen." New Age advocates instruct us to find strength by "looking within ourselves." Psychology tells us to feel good about ourselves. Religious people say that God will take us to heaven "if we are good."

In the midst of all this information, what should we believe? Where do we take our stand so that we are not tossed to and fro by the distorted information offered by the devil, the world, and our own sinful nature? Are we going to build our lives upon the shifting sands of human ideas and explanation and collapse in a heap when the adverse winds and tides of life come against us, or will we build our lives on the solid foundation of God's truth as revealed to us in his Son Jesus Christ and be able to stand in the midst of adversity?

Deceived by Words

It is not strange that we are living in a world of emotionally sick people. Negative attitudes, anxiety, depression, and adverse behavior are caused by the flood of wrong information that is received, mentally processed, and accepted as truth. Our lives are affected by what we believe. For this reason Jesus said that if we know the truth, the truth will make us free. I wholeheartedly agree with the principles of the *Misbelief Therapy* taught by Christian counselor Bill Backus. He writes in his very popular book *Telling Yourself the Truth:*

> Our feelings are not caused by the circumstances of our long-lost childhood or the circumstances of the present. *Our feelings are caused by what we tell ourselves about our circumstances*, whether in words or in attitudes.[1]

God has not left us alone in this world to sort things out for ourselves or to embrace every new fad or idea that the world throws at us. He sent his Son into our world to give his life for us so that we might be his sons and daughters and live under him in his kingdom. We have been given the eternal, enduring Word, the Holy Bible. In the pages of the Bible we discover what God has done for us, what he promises to do for us, and how he accomplishes those purposes. We know from the Bible what God thinks and says about this world, how he feels toward us, how we are to regard the negative circumstances of life, and what our future and destiny will be. God's Word will never deceive us.

For a Christian not to know and use God's Word and promises in the midst of a confusing world is a real tragedy. Where else can security, assurance, and hope for the future be found? God has given us the Bible so that we can live by his words and promises.

Talking to Yourself

The Word of God is very practical. When we memorize and are able to recall key verses of Scripture which declare the results of what God has accomplished for us in Christ and speak of God's wonderful promises for us his children, we are enabled to live and walk in victory. We become *overcomers*, not victims of our past or present adversities. To speak the Word in the midst of temptation, to meditate upon the Word and promise of God when passing through difficult circumstances, stirs within us the peace of God and keeps our hearts and our minds in Christ Jesus. Martin Luther wrote, "Hear God's Word often; do not go to bed, do not get up, without having spoken a beautiful passage—two, three, or four of them—to your heart."[2]

Clinical psychologist Albert Ellis developed in the early 1950's a therapy based upon the concept of self-talk. Ellis concluded that the reason why many of his patients did not get well is that they held irrational, self-defeating ideas about themselves. They had the wrong information. In order to change people, according to Ellis, it was necessary to change the information. Ellis concluded that human beings were verbal creatures who would silently, through the course of the day, talk to themselves. In his therapy he would instruct people to speak to themselves positive affirmations and to avoid speaking harmful, irrational, self-defeating words.[3]

By declaring and speaking to ourselves the message of God's grace, love, and forgiveness in Christ and reminding ourselves of his great and many promises, we are not merely embracing new information, but we are actually stirring up the very presence of God within us. The Holy Spirit works in us through Gospel promises found in the Bible. He opens our eyes and makes those promises real and practical.

As a result of consciously meditating upon the words and promises of God, we can daily experience the love, peace, and joy which is rightfully ours in Christ. Standing upon the promises of God will transform our lives. Our attitudes will be different. Our emotions will be stabilized by God's unchanging truth. Our relationships with others will be influenced by the great love with which God has loved us. The negative influences of the past will be swallowed by our glorious hope for the future.

Speaking Against Temptation

Taking a stand upon the Word and promises of God and declaring, "I am forgiven. I am right with God. I am going to heaven. I am more than a conqueror. Everything in my life is working out for good" is not without problems. As the result of taking a stand upon God's promises, we become susceptible to the temptations of the devil.

The person who believes nothing and simply goes with the flow of popular ideas of the day will not experience the temptation of the devil. After all, such a person is harmless in witnessing to the power of the Gospel and his life is probably so messed up already that there is no reason for the devil to waste his time with him.

Many Christians are confused over the work of the devil. While they are often enticed by the things of this world or by the desires of their own sinful nature, it is not the task of the devil to merely lead them into sin. Is it not true that after Adam and Eve sinned, we read very little about the devil in the Old Testament? Even though God's people were still tempted to fall into sin, such temptation emanated from their own sinful nature or from the sins of the nations that surrounded them.

It is the primary task of the devil to remove from us the Word of God, primarily the good news of the Gospel. He attacks our faith. In the parable of the sower, our Lord Jesus identified the birds who steal the newly sown seed as the devil. He does not want us to believe, confess, and stand upon the Word of God.

After Jesus was baptized, the Bible tells us that the Spirit led him into the wilderness to be tempted by the devil. And what was the target of the devil's temptation? At Christ's baptism God said, "You are my beloved Son." The devil, seeking to destroy this word of God, approached Jesus with the question "If you are the Son of God . . ." Jesus responded to all the temptations of the devil by speaking the Word of God: "Man does not live by bread alone!" "You shall not put the Lord your God to the test!" "You shall worship the Lord your God, and him only you shall serve!" Jesus did not argue with the devil. He simply declared, "Thus saith the Lord!"

The Bible refers to itself as the Sword of the Spirit, a sharp two-edged sword by which the temptations of the devil are defeated. If we are plagued by temptations that are leveled at our faith, we too should use the words of the Bible. In the midst of growing pessimism we declare: "My God is able to do immeasureably more than I ask or imagine! (from Ephesians 3:20). When faced by need we proclaim: "My God will meet all my needs according to his glorious riches in Christ Jesus!" (from Philippians 4:19). In the midst of worry or fear we speak forth: "If God is for me, who can be against me?" (from Romans 8:31). In times of weakness we confess: "I can do everything through him who gives me strength!" (from Philippians 4:13). In the midst of tragic situations or when confronted with the negative events that plagued our past, we say: "In all things God works for the good of those who love him, who have been called according to his purpose" (Romans 8:28). When we are feeling sad and forlorn, we say to ourselves: "Rejoice in the Lord always. I will say it again: Rejoice!" (from Philippians 4:4).

By speaking these words we are not merely affirming nice, sweet, positive ideas which are not in line with reality. Instead, we are declaring to the principalities and powers, to Satan and his host of demons, to the desires of our old sinful nature, to worry, fear, bitterness, resentment, to the events and circumstances of the past:

"Thus saith the Lord!" The Apostle Paul writes in 2 Corinthians 1:20, "No matter how many promises God has made, they are 'Yes' in Christ. And so through him, the 'Amen' is spoken by us to the glory of God." God's promises toward us are secure in Christ Jesus. By faith, in the midst of the adversities of life, we declare our Amen! to the truth of those promises.

I have known Christians who tape little "motto cards" to the refrigerator door. Each little card expresses a specific, edifying, biblical truth or promise. Every time they open the refrigerator, they are confronted with a meaningful passage from the Word of God.

The Powerful, Practical Word of God

When we compare what God has given us with the gimmicks, devices, and techniques of other religions or spiritual movements, we might think that we got "the short end of the stick," so to speak. Hindus can practice their meditation and experience inner illumination. Buddhists claim to find god within themselves. Even Islam seems more exciting, with its fastings, pilgrimages, and holy wars. New Agers and occultists have their astrology, pyramids, crystals, visualization, and the like. And Christians? What do we have? Well, our God has written us a Book.

Because we have an ancient Book from which we develop our doctrines and theologies, Christianity might be considered quite stuffy when compared to other religions. Founders of the new popular cults have attempted to add spice to Christianity with their new revelations. Joseph Smith claimed to find his edition of the Book of Mormon under a rock in New York State. Mary Baker Eddy wrote a key to the Scriptures so that her followers could "scientifically" interpret Scripture. The Moonies and the Jehovah's Witnesses add their little twists to Scripture to make it a little more exciting and interesting.

It is certainly true that, while other religions have their gimmicks and techniques, visions and mystical experiences, our God has written us a Book, *but what a Book it is!*

Is the Bible boring and stuffy? When you get to heaven, ask Martin Luther and John Calvin what they think. These are men who have been involved in the great reformations and revivals of the past. Each discovered that God has miraculously joined his own life-changing Spirit to his almighty and enduring Word. The Word of God transformed their own lives and the lives of literally millions after them. For me, my little Lithuanian grandmother who is in heaven is my role model. Because she faithfully read and meditated upon the Word of God every day, her life reflected profound joy, peace, and contentment.

Do you know people who are faithfully into the Word of God? If you do, examine their lives. Talk to them. Are they negative and bitter? Do they see themselves as victims of circumstances? Are they battered by the haunting memories of the events in their past? Are they concerned by their lack of self-esteem? Do they read self-help books and run to counselors? Hardly! Their lives have been transformed by the Word of God.

The worries, fears, anxieties, and emotional problems that you experience in your life are the result of a lack of understanding and proper use of God's Word and promises. You might read your self-help books, run to counselors to embrace quick fix solutions, and pray fervently that God would change your life, but without the Word of God, nothing happens.

If you are sick and tired of the ever-changing theories of psychology, if you are fed up with applying Band-Aids when surgery is required, if you are disappointed by your support groups and frustrated by your recovery programs, *try the Word of God through the enlightenment of the Holy Spirit.*

I guarantee, you will no longer be disappointed!

Notes

CHAPTER 2—THE SEARCH BEGINS

1. Watchman Nee, *The Normal Christian Life* (Fort Washington: Christian Literature Crusade, 1957), p. 9.

CHAPTER 3—WHAT HAPPENED TO ME?

1. John Calvin, *Institutes of the Christian Religion* (Grand Rapids: Eerdmans, 1983), Vol. II, pp. 240-1.
2. Ewald Plass, *What Luther Says* (St. Louis: Concordia Publishing House, 1959), Vol. III p. 1226.

CHAPTER 5—ENLIGHTENED BY THE HOLY SPIRIT

1. Edward T. Welch, *Counselor's Guide to the Brain and Its Disorders*, (Grand Rapids: Zondervan Publishing House, 1991), p. 34.
2. William Backus and Marie Chapman, *Telling Yourself the Truth*, (Minneapolis: Bethany House Publishers, 1980), p. 16.

CHAPTER 6—INSPIRATION AND ENLIGHTENMENT

1. Plass, *Luther,* Vol. I, p. 76.

CHAPTER 7—ASK, AND IT SHALL BE GIVEN YOU!

1. Heinrich Schmid, *The Doctrinal Theology of the Evangelical Lutheran Church* (Minneapolis: Augsburg Publishing House, 1875), p. 455.
2. Robert D. Preus, *The Theology of Post-Reformation Lutheranism* (St. Louis: Concordia Publishing House, 1970), pp. 219-20.
3. Calvin, *Institutes*, p. 37.

CHAPTER 8—SIN AND GRACE

1. Plass, *Luther*, Vol. III, p. 1293.
2. Paul Tournier, *Guilt and Grace* (New York: Harper and Row, 1959), pp. 159-60.
3. Robert Schuller, *Self-Esteem: The New Reformation* (Waco: Word, 1982), p. 98.
4. Ray S. Anderson, *The Gospel According to Judas* (Colorado Springs: Helmer and Howard, 1991), p. 99.
5. Calvin, *Institutes*, Vol. I, p. 211.
6. John D. Carter and Bruce Narramore, *The Integration of Psychology and Theology* (Grand Rapids: Zondervan, 1979), p. 11.
7. Dr. Gary Collins, *Can You Trust Psychology?* (Downers Grove: InterVarsity Press, 1988), p. 95.
8. David E. Roberts, *Existentialism and Religious Belief* (New York: Oxford University Press, 1959), p. 114.

9. Werner Elert, *The Structure of Lutheranism* (St. Louis: Concordia Publishing House, 1962), p. 18.

CHAPTER 10—THE MYSTERIOUS GOSPEL

1. Calvin, *Institutes,* Vol. 1, p. 364.
2. Plass, *Luther,* Vol. II, p. 562.
3. Ibid., p. 566.

CHAPTER 12—GOD GIVES, FAITH RECEIVES

1. Plass, *Luther,* Vol. I, p. 209.
2. Plass, *Luther,* Vol. II, p. 468.
3. Calvin, *Institutes,* p. 475.

CHAPTER 13—THE BIBLE IS REALLY TRUE!

1. Billy Graham, *The Holy Spirit* (Waco: Word Books, 1978), p. 44.
2. Calvin, *Institutes,* Vol. 1, pp. 72-73.
3. Trans. Everett Meier, *Convention Essays of C.F.W. Walther* (St. Louis: Concordia Publishing House, 1989), p. 10.

CHAPTER 14—WHERE DO WE BEGIN?

1. In addition to the Gospel, the theology of the Reformation also identified the Sacraments, namely Baptism and the Lord's Supper, as *means of grace.* While all Protestant Christians agree on the effective work of the Gospel of Jesus Christ, not all agree over the nature and effect of the Sacraments. While it is not my purpose to promote a specific denominational posture over against the transforming power of God's grace, let it suffice to say that I believe that many Christians hinder the power of grace by minimizing the effect of the Sacraments. When Christians come to the realization that their lives are ultimately products of grace, and not mere products of their faith or decision to accept grace, they will begin to see what the Sacraments really offer and deliver. To this end, I commit you to the Holy Spirit.
2. Plass, *Luther,* Vol II, p. 989.

CHAPTER 15—CHEWING ON THE WORD

1. Schmid, *Theology,* p. 454

CHAPTER 16—FACTS, NOT FEELINGS

1. Schmid, *Theology,* p. 457.
2. Graham, *Holy Spirit,* p. 46.
3. William Hordern, *Experience and Faith* (Minneapolis: Augsburg Publishing House, 1983), p. 44.

CHAPTER 17—PASTORS, THEOLOGIANS, AND CHURCH CUSTODIANS

1. Trans. and ed. Theodore Tappert, *The Book of Concord* (Philadelphia: Fortress Press, 1959), p. 574.

CHAPTER 18—WORDS TO LIVE BY

1. Backus and Chapman, *Truth,* p. 17.
2. Plass, *Luther,* Vol. III, p. 1485.
3. Gary Collins, *Your Magnificent Mind* (Grand Rapids: Baker Book House, 1988), p. 19.